Lush
LOW FAT
Desserts

MW01004691

Marie Oser

Foreword by Scott W. Sanders, Ph.D.

Chariot Publishing, Inc.

Editor: David Joachim
Cover Design and Illustration: Bonita Fladger-Wadell
Page Design: Diane M. Albeck
Photography: Guy Cali Associates, Inc.

Cover photo: Chocolate Blackout Cake

Chariot Publishing, Inc.
2 Public Avenue
Montrose, Pennsylvania 18801

First Printing: 1994

Library of Congress
Cataloging-in-Publication Data

Oser, Marie, date.
    Luscious low-fat desserts / Marie Oser; foreword by Scott W. Sanders
        p. cm.
    Includes index.
    ISBN 0-9622565-7-9 : $11.95
    1. Desserts. 2. Low-fat diet–Recipes. I. Title.
TX773.O84 1994
641.8'6–dc20   94-26004
                                                          CIP
            ISBN 0-9622565-7-9

The nutritional analyses in this book were calculated per serving and are based on the number of servings or serving size listed with each recipe. Calculations are rounded off to the nearest gram. If two options for an ingredient are listed, the first one is used. Calculations do not include oil or oil spray used for lubricating baking pans.

Contents

"Is it possible to create gourmet desserts without eggs, cream, butter or added fats... and get delicious results? Yes it is! Marie Oser shows you how."

— JOHN ROBBINS, Founder of EarthSave non-profit environmental organization, author of *May All Be Fed* and *Diet for a New America*

"As a pastry chef with traditional French training, I was amazed at the results I achieved using Marie's recipes. The Chocolate Blackout Cake is an incredibly moist, flavorful dessert that I couldn't seem to make enough of."

— CHRISTOPHE MARQUANT, Award-Winning Pastry Chef, Hotel Intercontinental, Los Angeles

"Decadent and exciting desserts that are low in fat without sacrificing flavor or texture? I didn't believe it until I tried a few of Marie's recipes. She's done it! It's a great book with lots of helpful tips. I recommend it."

— LYNN FISCHER, television host of *The Low Cholesterol Gourmet*, author of *The Quick Low Cholesterol Gourmet* and *Healthy Indulgences*

"Here is a cookbook I can recommend without reservation. I believe it should be a part of everyone's kitchen. With the increasing move toward low-fat diets, many people believe that desserts are no longer acceptable. Not so! Luscious Low-Fat Desserts offers a variety of truly delicious goodies without added fat, eggs or dairy products."

— SUSAN SMITH JONES, PH.D., author of *Choose to Be Healthy* and *Choose to Live Each Day Fully*

"Marie Oser has given us the best collection of delectable, rich-tasting desserts we've seen. The fact that they are healthy is merely a wonderful bonus. We plan to use these recipes in our own kitchen and to recommend them to clients."

— MARK MESSINA, PH.D. and VIRGINIA MESSINA, M.P.H., R.D., authors of *The Simple Soybean and Your Health*

Acknowledgements

My gratitude goes out to everyone at Chariot Publishing: Christiane Meunier for believing in me; Jessica Dubey for her guidance; Sue Van Nostrand for her invaluable assistance; and particularly Dave Joachim, a terrific editor whose skill, patience, flexibility and humor during countless hours of phoning and faxing coast to coast, developing and refining this book, proved indispensible.

Special thanks to my son, Justin, my very own "kitchen police." His interest in nutrition and his dedication to the principles of a strictly vegetarian diet, have been personally inspiring. He has been a primary "taster" and a strong asset to my work.

Thanks also to Russ Bianchi, a biochemist from FruitSource® and a valuable source of information. He explained to me on many occasions the chemistry underlying the success of my trial-and-error kitchen science.

My deepest thanks and heartfelt appreciation go to Mary Lisardi of Mary Lisardi and Associates. She singlehandedly worked through some very complicated software problems with the manuscript. She is truly a "computer maven."

And thanks to all my "tasters": Pat Moore, Ellen Tarentino, Judy Rae, Dale Hallcom and the gang at Earth News, Mary Kay and everyone at KNJO 92.7 FM Thousand Oaks, Rosemary Campagna and especially my daughter Kyra (for whom dessert could be the first and only course). It is for people like you, that this book is written.

This book is dedicated to my husband, Lanny,
without whose love, support and encouragement,
this effort would not have been possible.

Foreword

"I don't eat sweets often, but when I do, I want the real thing!"
"Why reduce fat?"

These are just two of the many comments I constantly hear about eating dessert.

Now for some heart-shattering facts:

- Over 1/3 of our children are overweight
- Our children's cholesterol averages 165... it should be about 140
- 98% of our children have at least one heart disease risk factor

Now that's scary and sad.

I first became acquainted with the work of Marie Oser through my involvement with the California Prune Board. As their technical research consultant, I had performed extensive investigative work on the ability of dried plums (prunes) to replace all or at least some of the fat in baked goods—without sacrificing flavor or texture. The prune butter or prune purée worked like a charm. In fact, these new, low-fat goodies were actually better than the "real" thing! Imagine eating a tablespoon of pure shortening... not too appetizing is it?

To my delight, Marie was already a pro at using not only dried plums, but also many other commonly available natural ingredients to replace fat. She had long since discovered that mother nature has created some of the best and most nourishing ingredients of all. Marie's recipes not only replace the fat, they actually *add* valuable nutrients such as dietary fiber, vitamins and minerals! Her recipes are easy to follow and even easier to make.

I'm convinced that one day large, commercial manufacturers will flock in droves to up-scale her methods to produce low-fat, wholesome and healthy supermarket offerings. This, of course, will make it more convenient for those who have difficulty finding the time to bake. But for those who love home-baked goods and homemade desserts, these are absolutely the best nonfat and low-fat recipes available.

You owe it to yourself—and to your family—to try these recipes. Your heart will thank you!

Scott W. Sanders, Ph.D.

Introduction

I first ventured into the kitchen when I was 12 years old. A box of Bisquick® and some interesting fillings were my tools. "Mix, roll, bake and serve." I'll never forget the pride I felt when my family gobbled up my treats and asked for more. Soon I was making quickbreads, cakes and cookies. I was hooked!

I have always enjoyed entertaining. Cooking and baking delicious food for family and friends has become a constant source of pleasure for me. A penchant for fine food soon developed into a serious interest in diet and nutrition. "You are what you eat" became a recurring phrase in my head. As information on health and nutrition became more available, I began to consider diet a crucial component of overall health and well-being. In turn, I increased my commitment to cutting the fat and refined sugar from my diet.

Without a doubt, dessert has been one of the biggest culprits in fat intake. Desserts derive their richness from two main sources: butter, shortening or oils and dairy products such as eggs, milk and cream. These ingredients contribute exorbitant amounts of fat and cholesterol to your diet.

For over two years, I have been refining and developing the use of alternatives to fat and dairy products in baked goods and chilled desserts. The results have been fantastic. These luscious desserts have lost nothing in the translation. Nothing— that is—except fat, calories and cholesterol. My family and many "tasters" have enjoyed every step of the development process. The result is *Luscious Low-Fat Desserts*, a cookbook that seriously addresses the fat/calorie/cholesterol issue without sacrificing the sensuous pleasure you expect from truly indulgent desserts.

How is it done? The key ingredients are frozen juice concentrate, fruit purées, egg replacer, Sucanat®, FruitSource®, soy milk lite and lite silken tofu. Mori-Nu® lite silken tofu has worked wonders in these desserts. Its silky, smooth texture is perfect for replacing eggs and dairy products in baked goods. It forms the basis of countless creamy pies and luscious icings in the book. It even helps to create a tender and tasty pie crust! These and other easy-to-use substitutes reduce the fat content of desserts well below 4 grams per serving (a few of the recipes here clock in at exactly 4 grams per serving). And since these desserts taste so outrageous, you can enjoy seconds— without regrets!

The ingredients recommended here are available in supermarkets and natural food stores across the country. For unfamiliar ingredients, consult the "Glossary of Ingredients," starting on page 13, which gives a brief description of each ingredient, indicating its use and availability. If any ingredient is unavailable to you locally, refer to the "Resource Guide" on page 119 for mail-order information.

I encourage you to take advantage of the available alternatives and techniques outlined here. With these delectable desserts, you can indulge your penchant for sweets and enjoy the benefits of a low-fat diet.

A Word About Substitutions

Throughout the recipes in this book, I have indicated substitutions for unfamiliar ingredients. For instance, brown rice syrup is offered as a substitute for FruitSource®, egg whites are offered as a substitute for egg replacer and water, brown sugar may replace Sucanat® and low-fat milk may be used in place of soy milk lite.

These substitutions are offered to make this cookbook as user-friendly as possible. However, the nutritional analyses are calculated using the first ingredient listed, i.e. FruitSource, egg replacer and water, or Sucanat. The first ingredient listed is the ingredient of choice. It is the one that I recommend to create these fabulous desserts. In no way do I endorse the use of eggs, dairy products or honey. These substitutions are offered solely for the reader's convenience.

For those who may prefer honey as a substitute for the liquid sweeteners, a 1:1 ratio is a good rule of thumb. However, due to water activity, seasonality, source of pollen, etc., honey may vary in sweetness, taste and texture. Be aware of these variances when substituting honey for a listed ingredient. Also, honey is actually higher in calories than sugar.

A Note About Cooking Time

Cooking and preparation times are listed for each recipe as "Total Time." This allows time for preparation, cooking, baking and assembly but, in some cases, does not include cooling, refrigeration or freezing time.

Techniques

The Basics

It is important to note some basic information that will provide the novice dessert baker with "know how" and remind the experienced baker of rudimentary elements.

- **Always** read all the way through a recipe before proceeding. Make sure you have all of the required ingredients and utensils. It is frustrating to start a recipe and then have to run out for a key ingredient. Of course, if you are an experienced cook, you may have your own substitutes.
- Flour should be measured with a measuring cup and leveled off by dragging a butterknife across the top. Most cookbooks will tell you to spoon flour into a measuring cup. I use a measuring cup with a handle, scooping the flour loosely and then leveling off. Never pack the flour down into the cup.
- While very experienced cooks can "eyeball" the proper measure, it is important to use the exact measure when baking. In particular, leavening agents must be measured accurately to ensure successful results. Use measuring spoons and cups rather than spoons and cups designed for dining.
- When measuring liquid ingredients, a glass measuring cup will allow you to see the liquid more accurately. When using liquid sweeteners, it is a good idea to heat the liquid slightly. I heat FruitSource and other fruit sweeteners for 10 to 15 seconds in the microwave—right in the glass measuring cup. This will make the liquid more fluid so you will be able to get it all out of the cup.
- Measure the dry ingredients first to save you the time and hassle of washing and drying the wet measuring utensils between uses.
- When using brown sugar, measuring cups with handles are the best choice. Scoop out the desired amount from the package and pack it down firmly. When using Sucanat, there is no need to pack it down since the texture is more like sugar.
- When using lite silken tofu, always blend it until smooth by itself, before adding the other ingredients.

Working with Phyllo Dough

Phyllo dough is readily available in the freezer section of most supermarkets. It should be placed in the refrigerator the night before the day you intend to use it and brought to room temperature in the package 2 to 4 hours before use. Remove the number of sheets needed and freeze the remainder in the package.

Always make the filling before removing the phyllo from its wrapper. If the filling has been cooked, it should be cooled before mounding it onto the prepared layers of phyllo. This will prevent the dough from becoming soggy. To promote crispness, sweet-flavored breadcrumbs should be sprinkled between the layers of phyllo dough.

If you've never worked with these leaves of dough, you might think they are sheets of translucent paper. They are very delicate and dry out easily, so they should be handled gingerly. While working quickly with each individual layer, keep the remaining dough covered with a damp cloth. I like to use a water spritzer, like the typical indoor plant sprayer, to keep the cloth from drying out while I work. Generally the leaves of phyllo dough are brushed with melted butter, before placement, to promote flakiness. In my approach to low-fat desserts, I have used an oil-mist spray instead. There are butter-flavored mists on the market, but this flavor is not absolutely necessary, especially if you do not include butter in your regular diet. In this and other instances, the use of pan sprays has proven to cut the fat significantly with successful end results.

Food Processing Techniques

Throughout this book I have made full use of the food processor. I have found it to be an indispensible cooking tool for streamlining preparation time. However, indications are always made for alternative appliances such as blenders and mixers where applicable.

Several recipes direct you to use a "pulse technique." This technique allows you to process ingredients to a crumbly consistency in a short amount of time. Many food processors include a pulse button. For those without a pulse button, simply "pulse" the on/off switch (turn it on and off in rapid succession) until ingredients are crumbly. For blenders and mixers, use the highest setting and turn the appliance on and off in rapid succession until ingredients are crumbly.

When making frozen desserts, I use the food processor method of preparation. First purée the frozen dessert ingredients, freeze for 4 hours, then purée a second time and return the dessert to the freezer for 20 minutes before serving. Leftover frozen desserts will probably need to be re-processed briefly before serving. Process only to restore an ice cream-like consistency, using the pulse technique. Do not liquefy.

Folding Techniques

When a recipe calls for ingredients to be combined alternately with vanilla rice milk or a soy "buttermilk" mixture, the dry ingredients should be added first and last to the liquid ingredients in three steps. In other words, the liquid mixture is folded in between in two steps as follows:

Step 1: dry ingredients
Step 2: liquid ingredients
Step 3: dry ingredients
Step 4: liquid ingredients
Step 5: dry ingredients

Frosting Layer Cakes

Before frosting a layer cake, be sure that both the cake and icing are completely cool. The cake layers should be free of loose crumbs. Use a flat serving plate that is at least two inches wider in diameter than the cake to be frosted. Cut four strips of wax paper, about 4" wide. Cover the edges of the plate with the wax paper strips, forming a square. This will keep the plate free of drips.

Choose the thickest cake layer for the bottom and center it on the plate, resting it on the wax paper, top-side down. If the cake is especially rounded, use a long bladed serrated knife and shave off a thin slice in order to steady the cake. This will eliminate the gaps that sometimes occur between layers.

Using a long metal spatula, cover the bottom layer with icing (or filling) to within 1/2" of the outer edge. Center the second layer over the first, top-side up, and frost to within 1/2" of the outer edge. (If you are working with a three-layer cake, repeat the layering procedure, leveling off the second layer as you did the first. Place the third layer, top-side up, on top of the second layer.)

Holding the spatula vertically, frost the sides lightly with a thin layer of icing. Next spread the icing along the top edge and down along the sides. Place the remaining frosting in the center of the top layer of cake and spread outward with a swirling motion, filling in around the sides as you go. If desired, decorate with fresh fruit or sprinkles.

After the icing has been allowed to set, lift the cake gently along the edge with a metal spatula and carefully remove the wax paper strips.

Icing Yields

The following list is intended as a general guide and icing yields are approximated.

To Frost:	You will need:
top and sides of a 2-layer cake	2 1/2 cups
top and sides of a 3-layer cake	3 cups
top of one 9" x 5" loaf cake	3/4 cup
top of one 9" x 13" cake	2 1/3 cups

Glossary of Ingredients

Agar flakes (agar-agar, sea vegetable flakes)—a colorless, odorless, tasteless, and calorie-free gelling agent used to replace gelatin (which is an animal product). It is available in several forms (such as bars) in natural food stores. In this book, I have used agar flakes only. They are the easiest to work with.

Apple butter—an excellent fat replacer in baked goods, especially spice cakes. It is made from fresh apples and is available in natural food stores. I use only unsweetened apple butter in these recipes.

Barley malt syrup—a natural sweetener used interchangeably with honey or other liquid sweeteners. It is available in natural food stores.

Brown rice syrup—a thick, sweet syrup used interchangeably with honey or other liquid sweeteners. It is available in natural food stores.

Canola oil—a light-colored, flavorless oil which is a mono-unsaturated fat. It is a good plant-based source of Omega-3 fatty acids.

Canola oil mist—a non-aerosol pan spray used in place of oils and shortenings to lubricate baking pans. It is available in large supermarkets and natural food stores. It can also be used in baking (*see* Easy Apple Strudel on page 43).

Carob powder (St. John's bread, johnny bread)—a dark brown cocoa-like powder used in place of chocolate. It is ground from a highly nutritious bean that has half the fat of cocoa and contains no caffeine.

Date nuggets (date pieces)—chopped dates that have been rolled in oat flour rather than sugar. They are available in large supermarkets and natural food stores.

Date sugar—a substitute for brown sugar made from ground dates. It can be expensive. I prefer to use Sucanat, an unrefined form of sugar cane juice which has produced excellent results.

Egg replacer—a powdered leavening and binding agent used as a substitute for eggs in baked goods. It is a flour made from tapioca and potato starch and is available in natural food stores.

FruitSource®—a substitute for honey or sugar in baked goods. This natural sweetener is made from grapes and grains and is available in natural food stores in both liquid and granulated form.

Gingerroot—a knobby root with a spicy flavor. It is available in supermarkets, greengrocers and natural food stores. Fresh gingerroot is usually peeled and grated for use in dessert recipes.

Just Like Shortenin'™—a new product used to replace traditional high-fat shortenings. It is made from plums and apples and is becoming widely available. (If this product is unavailable to you locally, refer to the "Resource Guide" on page 119 for mail order information.)

Leavening agents—substances that produce a gas to lighten or raise dough or batter. Non-aluminum baking powder, baking soda and cream of tartar are all leavening agents available in supermarkets and natural food stores.

Lite silken tofu—a reduced-fat form of silken tofu. It is sold in aseptic packages in large supermarkets and natural food stores. Lite silken tofu has 75% less fat than regular silken tofu and does not sacrifice flavor or texture. (*See also* Silken tofu.)

Maple syrup—a popular substitute for honey in baked goods. Always use 100% pure maple syrup. It is available in supermarkets and natural food stores.

Millers bran—an unprocessed wheat bran derived from the outside shell of the whole bran. It is the most common form of bran available and is used to boost the fiber content in baked goods. It is available in supermarkets and natural food stores.

Multi-blend flour—a blend of flours milled from a variety of whole grains and legumes, including whole grain wheat flour, whole grain barley flour, pinto bean flour, green lentil flour, whole millet flour and whole grain rye flour. It has its origins in biblical times.

Mystic Lake® fruit sweetener—a liquid sweetener used to replace honey in baked goods. It is available in natural food stores.

Natural applesauce—a very effective fat substitute in baked goods. I use only natural unsweetened applesauce.

Oat bran—a fiber-rich bran derived from oats. It adds a distinctive hearty flavor to baked goods.

Orzo—small, rice-shaped pasta available in most supermarkets.

Phyllo dough—paper-thin sheets of dough used in pastries. Phyllo dough is readily available in the freezer section of most supermarkets.

Prune butter (Lekvar)—a fat replacer made from puréed prunes and a small amount of sweetener such as corn syrup.

Prune purée—a homemade fat replacer used interchangeably with prune butter in baked goods. To make prune purée, place 2 cups of pitted prunes, 3/4 cup water and 4 teaspoons vanilla extract in a food processor or blender. Blend until smooth. Refrigerate in a covered container for up to two weeks.

Rice milk—a delicious non-dairy beverage with a mildly sweet flavor that can be used in place of dairy milk and soy milk. The Rice Dream® brand is available in both original (plain) or vanilla flavors and contains 1% fat and no cholesterol.

Silken tofu—a smooth-textured, custard-like tofu that is sold in aseptic packages and is available in most supermarkets and natural food stores. Like regular tofu it is made from soybeans. Silken tofu is an effective egg substitute when used in 1/4 cup tofu to one egg proportions. It is available in soft, firm and extra firm consistencies. I prefer the extra firm consistency. (*See also* Lite silken tofu.)

Soy buttermilk—a good substitute for dairy buttermilk in baked goods. It is made by adding 2 tablespoons of lemon juice to 1 cup of soy milk.

Soy milk lite—a reduced-fat soy milk that is 1% fat. It is available in large supermarkets and natural food stores.

Sucanat®—a granulated form of unrefined cane sugar made from organic sugar cane juice. It is a whole food that retains all of the vitamins and minerals provided by nature. It is not considered sugar, as that term implies a process of refining. This sweetener is stirred into the dry ingredients in baked goods, as it will not emulsify with the creamed ingredients. It can be used interchangeably with brown sugar and is available in natural food stores.

Unbleached all-purpose flour—a naturally white flour that has not been bleached, enriched or sifted.

Wheat germ—the most vital part of the wheat kernel. It is rich in protein, iron, vitamin B_1 and vitamin E.

Whole wheat flour—a wheat flour containing all of the wheat, including the bran and the germ.

Whole wheat pastry flour—the best flour for most baked goods. It is more finely milled than whole wheat flour and has a lower gluten content.

*Cinnamon, nutmeg and fresh almonds give Almond Streusel Cake (recipe on page 20) a delightfully sweet crunch with **only 3 grams of fat** per serving.*

Heavenly Torte Reform (recipe on page 30) redefines the meaning of dessert decadence. Bursting with the fresh flavor of raspberries and lemon, this moist, delicious cake has only **2 grams of fat** per serving!

Cakes

Do you crave the sensuous luxury of a truly extravagant dessert? A devilishly delectable confection that will end the meal with style and grace? Perhaps you think this sort of decadence is outside the realm of low-fat cuisine. Perhaps you have been told that fat-free and low-fat cakes are bland and lack flair. Well, look again. The cakes in this chapter are nothing short of indulgent.

You'll find recipes like Fudge Glazed Marble Ring, a moist and rich marble cake with a thick fudgy glaze. And why not dig in? It has only a gram of fat per serving and absolutely no cholesterol.

One way I achieve a rich cake without eggs or dairy is to use lite silken tofu. Its creamy, custard-like consistency is perfect for replacing the eggs and milk found in traditional cakes. And its low-fat profile will keep you coming back for seconds. Another secret is low-fat "buttermilk" made with soy milk lite and lemon juice. This soy buttermilk mixture produces the same great results in baked goods as dairy buttermilk—without the fat!

With these and other new substitutes for old, high-fat ingredients, you can be proud to serve these delicious, show-stopping desserts to your family and friends. For the chocolate lovers, serve Chocolate Blackout Cake, clocking in at just 2 grams of fat per serving. Even filled with Rich 'N Creamy Chocolate Pudding (as shown on the cover), it still has only 3 grams of fat per serving. Or enjoy the healthy new spin of classic desserts like Moist & Marvelous Carrot Cake and Austrian Apple Torte.

None of the cakes has over 3 grams of fat per serving. So indulge with confidence. These cakes will knock your socks off!

Almond Streusel Cake

For a festive presentation, fill the center of this bundt cake with a mound of fresh strawberries and dust with powdered sugar.

Total Time: 1 hour
Serves 16

1/2 cup chopped almonds
2 Tbsp. brown sugar
2 tsp. cinnamon
1/2 tsp. nutmeg
3 1/2 cups whole wheat
   pastry flour
1 1/2 tsp. baking soda
2 tsp. baking powder

1/2 tsp. salt
1 (10.5 oz.) pkg. lite silken tofu
   (extra firm)
1 cup vanilla rice milk or
   low-fat milk
1/2 cup natural applesauce
1 1/2 cups brown sugar
1 1/4 tsp. almond extract

Per serving: 218 cal, 6 g prot, 222 mg sod, 45 g carb, 3 g fat, 0 mg chol, 80 mg calcium

- Preheat oven to 375°F. Lightly oil a bundt pan.
- Chop nuts in food processor or blender. Blend in brown sugar, cinnamon and nutmeg to form streusel mixture. Set aside.
- Combine next 4 ingredients in a large bowl. Set aside.
- Blend tofu until smooth in food processor or mixing bowl. Blend in rice milk, applesauce, brown sugar and almond extract.
- Add tofu mixture to dry ingredients and mix to form batter.
- Pour half of batter into pan and sprinkle almond streusel mixture evenly over batter.
- Top with remaining batter and bake untill golden brown and toothpick inserted in center comes out clean, about 40 minutes.
- Cool in pan for 15 minutes. Invert onto wire rack and cool completely before serving.

Hint:

Rice Dream® is a brand of rice milk that is available in both plain and vanilla flavors. It is 1% fat.

Apple Apple Cake

*Cut this delicately spiced cake into squares
and serve with iced tea or lemonade.*

**Total Time: 1 hour
Serves 16**

8 cups peeled, sliced Granny
  Smith apples
2 Tbsp. lemon juice
2 1/4 cups whole wheat
  pastry flour
1/4 cup wheat germ
2 tsp. baking soda
1 tsp. baking powder
2 tsp. cinnamon

1/4 tsp. salt
1 cup unsweetened apple butter
2 cups brown sugar
2 Tbsp. egg replacer ⎱
1/2 cup cold water ⎰
  or 1/2 cup egg white
1 tsp. grated lemon rind
1 cup vanilla soy milk or low-fat milk

Per serving: 239 cal, 4 g prot, 176 mg sod, 58 g carb, 1 g fat, 0 mg chol, 68 mg calcium

- Preheat oven to 350°F. Lightly oil a 9" x 13" pan.
- Toss apples with lemon juice in a large bowl. Set aside.
- Combine next 6 ingredients in a medium-size bowl. Set aside.
- Cream apple butter and brown sugar in a large bowl.
- Whisk egg replacer with water until foamy and add to apple butter mixture. Blend in lemon rind.
- Add dry ingredients to liquid ingredients alternately with soy milk and mix to form batter.
- Spread apple slices evenly over bottom of pan and pour batter on top.
- Bake until a toothpick inserted in center comes out clean, about 35 minutes. Cool in pan. Cut and serve.

Hint:

*Dust with powdered
sugar for a decorative
presentation.*

Austrian Apple Torte

This elegant torte is easy to prepare and low in fat and calories.

Total Time: 1 hour
Serves 12

1 cup rolled oats
1 1/4 cups whole wheat
   pastry flour
1/4 tsp. salt
1/2 tsp. cinnamon
1 tsp. grated lemon rind
1/4 cup lite silken tofu
   (extra firm)
1 Tbsp. canola oil
1/4 cup liquid FruitSource® or
   brown rice syrup

1/4 cup ice water
4 cups cored, peeled,
   sliced apples*
1 Tbsp. grated lemon rind
3 Tbsp. unbleached
   all-purpose flour
1/4 cup Sucanat® or brown sugar
1 tsp. cinnamon
1/4 tsp. nutmeg
1/3 cup blackberry, strawberry
   or apricot jam

Per serving: 191 cal, 6 g prot, 67 mg sod, 39 g carb, 3 g fat, 0 mg chol, 15 mg calcium

- Preheat oven to 350°F. Lightly oil a spring form pan.
- Grind oats into oat flour in food processor or blender. Combine oat flour with next 4 ingredients.
- Mash tofu with a fork and blend into flour mixture. Add oil, FruitSource and water, mixing in each ingredient separately.
- When dough begins to form a ball, remove and press into disc shape with palm of hands. Place disc between two floured sheets of wax paper and roll into a circle 1/4" thick.
- Press dough into bottom of pan, gently coaxing dough 1 1/2" up sides to form a crust
- Toss apples with lemon rind, flour, Sucanat, cinnamon and nutmeg in a large bowl Arrange coated apple slices over dough.
- Warm jam for 15 seconds in microwave or 2 minutes in a saucepan over low heat. Drizzle over apples.
- Set pan on a cookie sheet. Bake on center rack of oven for 35 to 40 minutes. Cool in pan for 15 minutes.
- Refrigerate to cool completely (filling will harden). When torte is completely cool, unhinge the spring and lift off sides. Slide torte onto a serving plate.

Hint:

I prefer to use Granny Smith apples for their tartness, but any apple may be used.

Chocolate Blackout Cake

*Brandied apricots and a thick chocolate glaze
make this one of my favorite cakes.*

Total Time: 1 hour
Serves 12

1/4 cup apricot brandy
1 cup dried apricots, chopped
2 Tbsp. lemon juice ⎱
1 cup soy milk lite ⎰
   or 1 cup buttermilk
2 1/4 cups unbleached
   all-purpose flour
1 1/2 tsp. baking soda
1 1/2 tsp. baking powder
3/4 cup unsweetened
   cocoa powder

1 tsp. cinnamon
1 (10.5 oz.) pkg. lite silken tofu
   (extra firm)
1 tsp. vanilla extract
1/2 cup natural applesauce
1 3/4 cups brown sugar
1 cup apricot jam, preferably
   fruit sweetened
1 1/2 cups Fudgy Chocolate
   Glaze (recipe on page 92)

Per serving: 397 cal, 7 g prot, 228 mg sod, 90 g carb, 2 g fat, 0 mg chol, 83 mg calcium

- Preheat oven to 350°F. Lightly oil and flour three 9" round cake pans.
- Heat brandy in a small saucepan over low flame for 2 to 3 minutes. Add apricots and simmer until liquid is absorbed, about 3 minutes. Cover and set aside.
- Add lemon juice to soy milk and set aside.
- Sift next 5 ingredients in a medium-size bowl. Set aside.
- Blend tofu until smooth in food processor or mixing bowl. Blend in vanilla and set aside.
- Mix applesauce and brown sugar until smooth in a large bowl. Whisk in blended tofu.
- Add dry ingredients to liquid ingredients alternately with soy "buttermilk" mixture and mix to form batter. Fold in brandied apricots.
- Pour batter evenly into pans and bake until toothpick inserted in center comes out clean, about 30 minutes.
- Cool in pans for 10 minutes. Invert onto wire racks to cool completely.

To assemble:
- Spread apricot jam between each layer. Spoon glaze evenly over top, letting it drip down sides.

Hint:

*For a more decadent
cake (as shown on the
cover), fill with Rich 'N
Creamy Chocolate
Pudding (recipe on
page 106) instead
of apricot jam.
Decorate with a white
glaze by combining
1 cup sifted powdered
sugar, 1/4 teaspoon
vanilla and 1 1/2 table-
spoons rice milk.*

Chocolate Raspberry Roll

Turn any meal into an occasion with this sensational dessert topped with a rich Chocolate Raspberry Icing (recipe on page 87). Less than 1 gram of fat per serving!

Total Time: 1 hour
Serves 12

2 Tbsp. lemon juice ⎱
1 cup soy milk lite ⎰
   or 1 cup buttermilk
1 cup whole wheat pastry flour
1 cup Sucanat® or brown sugar
1/2 tsp. baking soda
1/2 tsp. baking powder
2/3 cup cocoa powder
1/4 tsp. salt
1/4 cup prune butter

1/3 cup frozen raspberry juice
   concentrate, thawed*
2 Tbsp. egg replacer ⎱
1/2 cup cold water ⎰
   or 1/2 cup egg white
1 tsp. vanilla extract
2 Tbsp. powdered sugar
2 1/4 cups Raspberry Maple Filling
   (recipe on page 95)
3 cups Chocolate Raspberry Icing
   (recipe on page 87)

Per serving: 182 cal, 5 g prot, 86 mg sod, 39 g carb, 0.9 g fat, 0 mg chol, 50 mg calcium

- Preheat oven to 375°F. Lightly oil a 10 1/2" x 15 1/2" jelly roll pan. Line pan with wax paper and lightly oil paper.
- Add lemon juice to soy milk and set aside.
- Combine next 6 ingredients in a medium-size bowl. Set aside.
- Blend prune butter and juice concentrate in a large bowl.
- Whisk egg replacer with water until foamy and add to juice mixture. Stir in vanilla.
- Add dry ingredients to liquid ingredients alternately with soy "buttermilk" mixture and mix to form batter. Spread batter evenly into pan and bake until toothpick inserted in center comes out clean, about 20 minutes.
- Dust a towel with powdered sugar. While cake is still hot, invert onto towel and peel off wax paper. With serrated knife or scissors, trim crusty edges.
- Wrap cake in towel and roll up around a rolling pin. Let cake cool in rolled position. When completely cool, unroll and unfold towel from inner side of cake. Spread filling evenly over inner side of cake.
- Reroll cake gently, removing towel as you roll. Place cake seam side down on a serving plate and frost with icing. Serve.

Hints:

*I use Dole® Country Raspberry frozen juice concentrate. It is a delicious mixture of raspberry, apple, pineapple and white grape juices.
See illustrations on page 25.

Rolling instructions for Chocolate Raspberry Roll

1) Place cake on towel that has been dusted with powdered sugar. Remove wax paper.
2) Fold towel over cake.

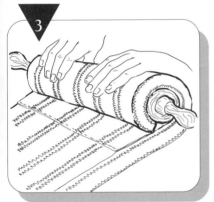 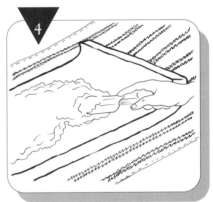

3) Roll cake and towel over rolling pin. 4) Unroll cake and spread evenly with filling.

5) Reroll filled cake, removing towel as you roll. 6) Place cake, seam-side down, on a serving plate and frost with icing.

Cranberry Spice Cake

*Tart cranberries and sweet spices are
an irresistible combination.*

Total Time: 1 hour
Serves 16

2 Tbsp. lemon juice ⎫
1 cup soy milk lite ⎭
   or 1 cup buttermilk
1 cup unbleached
   all-purpose flour
2 tsp. baking soda
1 tsp. baking powder
1 1/2 tsp. cinnamon
1/2 tsp. nutmeg
1 1/2 cups granulated
   FruitSource® or brown sugar

1 1/4 cups whole wheat pastry flour
1 cup unsweetened apple butter
1/2 cup brown sugar
2 Tbsp. egg replacer ⎫
1/2 cup cold water ⎭
   or 1/2 cup egg white
2 tsp. vanilla extract
1 tsp. grated lemon rind
1 (16 oz.) can whole berry
   cranberry sauce
1 cup golden raisins

Per serving: 210 cal, 3 g prot, 146 mg sod, 51 g carb, 0.5 g fat, 0 mg chol, 52 mg calcium

- Preheat oven to 400°F. Lightly oil a 9" x 13" pan.
- Add lemon juice to soy milk and set aside.
- Sift next 5 ingredients in a medium-size bowl. Stir in FruitSource and flour. Set aside.
- Cream apple butter and brown sugar in a large bowl.
- Whisk egg replacer with water until foamy and add to apple butter mixture. Whisk in vanilla and lemon rind.
- Add dry ingredients to liquid ingredients alternately with soy "buttermilk" mixture and mix to form batter.
- Spread cranberry sauce evenly across bottom of pan and sprinkle with raisins.
- Pour batter over fruit and bake until toothpick inserted in center comes out clean, about 30 minutes. Cool in pan. Cut and serve.

Fudge Glazed Marble Ring

*This moist marble cake, topped with a thick fudgy glaze, made
an elegant presentation on my daughter Kyra's 19th birthday.
And it has only 1 gram of fat per serving!*

**Total Time: 1 hour
Serves 16**

*2 Tbsp. lemon juice ⎫
1 cup soy milk lite ⎭
  or 1 cup buttermilk
3 1/2 cups unbleached
  all-purpose flour
1 1/2 tsp. baking soda
2 tsp. baking powder
1/4 tsp. salt
1 (10.5 oz.) pkg. lite silken tofu
  (extra firm)*

*2 tsp. vanilla extract
1 tsp. almond extract
1/3 cup natural applesauce
2 cups brown sugar
1/4 cup boiling water
3 Tbsp. cocoa powder
3/4 cup Fudgy Chocolate Glaze
  (recipe on page 92)*

Per serving: 248 cal, 5 g prot, 201 mg sod, 55 g carb, 1 g fat, 0 mg chol, 68 mg calcium

Preheat oven to 350°F. Lightly oil and flour a tube pan.

Add lemon juice to soy milk and set aside.

Sift next 4 ingredients in a medium-size bowl. Set aside.

Blend tofu until smooth in food processor or mixing bowl. Blend in vanilla and almond extracts. Set aside.

Mix applesauce and brown sugar until smooth in a large bowl. Whisk in tofu mixture gradually.

Add dry ingredients to liquid ingredients alternately with soy "buttermilk" mixture and mix to form batter.

Pour boiling water over cocoa powder in a medium-size bowl. Stir to form a smooth syrup.

Remove 1 1/2 cups of batter and blend into syrup. Set aside.

Pour half of vanilla batter into pan. Spoon chocolate batter in dollops over vanilla layer, leaving spaces of black and white. Spoon remaining vanilla batter in dollops over all, leaving spaces of black and white. *(See illustrations on page 28.)*

- Run a butter knife deeply through batters, swirling to create a marbling effect. Tap pan against side of counter to release air bubbles.
- Place pan on a cookie sheet in center rack of oven and bake until toothpick inserted in center comes out clean, about 40 minutes.
- Cool in pan. When completely cool, transfer to serving plate and spoon glaze evenly over top, letting drip down sides.

Hint:

If a tube pan is unavailable, a 12-cup bundt pan may be used.

Marbling instructions for Fudge Glazed Marble Ring

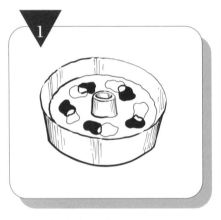 

1) Pour half of vanilla batter into tube pan. Top with dollops of chocolate batter and remaining vanilla batter, leaving spaces of black and white. 2) Run a butter knife deeply through batters, swirling to create marbling effect.

Hawaiian Sunset Cake

*Light as a tropical breeze, enchanting as a Maui sunset, this is
one dessert that will end any meal with sweet style.*

**Total Time: 45 min.
Serves 16**

1 cup canned crushed pineapple,
    packed in juice
1 1/2 cups rolled oats
1 cup unbleached
    all-purpose flour
1/2 cup chopped walnuts
1/2 cup wheat germ
2/3 cup Sucanat® or
    brown sugar
2 tsp. baking soda
1 tsp. baking powder
1 tsp. cinnamon

1/2 tsp. salt
1/2 cup natural applesauce
1/4 cup liquid FruitSource® or
    brown rice syrup
2 Tbsp. egg replacer }
1/2 cup cold water }
    or 1/2 cup egg white
1 tsp. vanilla extract
2/3 cup soy milk lite or low-fat milk
1 cup golden raisins
2 1/3 cups Island DeLite Icing
    (recipe on page 92)

Per serving: 162 cal, 7 g prot, 163 mg sod, 29 g carb, 3 g fat, 0 mg chol, 41 mg calcium

Preheat oven to 350°F. Lightly oil a 9" x 13" baking pan.

Drain pineapple, reserving juice for icing. Set aside.

Grind oats into oat flour in food processor or blender. Combine oat flour with next 8 ingredients in a medium-size bowl. Set aside.

Whisk applesauce and FruitSource in a large bowl.

Whisk egg replacer with water until foamy and add to applesauce mixture. Stir in vanilla and drained pineapple.

Add dry ingredients to liquid ingredients alternately with soy milk and mix to form batter. Fold in raisins.

Pour batter into pan and bake until toothpick inserted in center comes out clean, about 30 minutes. Cool in pan. When completely cool, frost with icing.

Heavenly Torte Reform

*This fabulous raspberry lemon torte is low in fat
and contains no sugar and no cholesterol.*

Total Time: 1 hour
Serves 16

1 cup rolled oats
3 cups whole wheat pastry flour
1 cup Sucanat® or brown sugar
1 1/2 tsp. baking soda
1 tsp. baking powder
1 (10.5 oz.) pkg. lite silken tofu
  (extra firm)
1/2 cup natural applesauce
1 Tbsp. grated lemon rind
1 tsp. lemon extract

1/4 cup lemon juice
1/2 cup liquid FruitSource® or brown
  rice syrup
1 cup vanilla rice milk or low-fat
  milk with 1/4 tsp. vanilla
2 1/4 cups Raspberry Maple Filling
  (recipe on page 95)
3 cups Lemon Yellow Icing (recipe on
  page 93)
2 cups fresh raspberries for garnish

Per serving: 270 cal, 9 g prot, 168 mg sod, 57 g carb, 2 g fat, 0 mg chol, 47 mg calcium

- Preheat oven to 350°F. Lightly oil three 8" round cake pans.
- Grind oats into oat flour in food processor or blender. Combine oat flour with next 4 ingredients in a large bowl. Set aside.
- Blend tofu until smooth in food processor or mixing bowl. Blend in next ingredients.
- Add tofu mixture to dry ingredients and mix to form batter.
- Pour batter evenly into three pans and bake for 25 to 30 minutes.
- Cool in pans for 10 minutes, turn onto racks and cool completely.

To assemble:
- Place one cake layer on serving platter and spread with half of filling to 1/2" of edge. Top with second layer and spread with remaining filling. Top with third layer and frost with icing.
- Garnish with fresh raspberries.

Hint:

*For cake assembly
tips, see "Frosting
Layer Cakes"
on page 11.*

Moist & Marvelous Carrot Cake

*Frosted with Lemon Yellow Icing (recipe on page 93),
this makes a festive birthday cake.*

**Total Time: 1 hour
Serves 12**

1 cup rolled oats
2 1/2 cups whole wheat
   pastry flour
1 1/2 tsp. baking soda
1 tsp. baking powder
1 tsp. cinnamon
1/2 cup natural applesauce
1 1/2 cups brown sugar

2 Tbsp. egg replacer }
1/2 cup cold water
   or 1/2 cup egg white
1/2 cup rice milk or low-fat milk
2 tsp. vanilla extract
2 cups coarsely grated carrots
1 cup golden raisins
3 cups Lemon Yellow Icing
   (recipe on page 93)

Per serving: 337 cal, 9 g prot, 181 mg sod, 74 g carb, 2 g fat, 0 mg chol, 96 mg calcium

Preheat oven to 350°F. Lightly oil two 8" or 9" round cake pans.

Grind oats into oat flour in food processor or blender. Combine oat flour with next 4 ingredients in a large bowl. Set aside.

Mix applesauce and brown sugar until smooth in a medium-size bowl.

Whisk egg replacer with water until foamy and add to applesauce mixture. Whisk in rice milk and vanilla.

Add liquid ingredients to dry ingredients and mix to form batter. Fold in carrots and raisins.

Pour batter evenly into pans and bake until toothpick inserted in center comes out clean, about 25 minutes.

Cool in pan for 10 minutes and turn onto wire racks to cool completely. When completely cool, transfer to a serving plate and frost evenly with icing.

Hint:

For cake assembly tips, see "Frosting Layer Cakes" on page 11.

Multi-Blend Snacking Cake

This delicious, wholesome cake is a wonderful addition to your child's lunchbox.

Total Time: 45 minutes
Serves 12

3/4 cup multi-blend flour*
1/4 cup wheat germ
1/2 cup millers bran
1 tsp. baking soda
3/4 tsp. baking powder
1/4 tsp. salt
1 tsp. cinnamon
1/2 cup Sucanat® or brown sugar
6 Tbsp. lite silken tofu (firm)
1 medium-size ripe banana, mashed

1/4 cup vanilla rice milk or
    low-fat milk
1/4 cup natural applesauce
1/4 cup liquid FruitSource® or
    brown rice syrup
1 tsp. vanilla extract
1/2 cup dark raisins
3 Tbsp. sunflower seeds
1/8 tsp. nutmeg

Per serving: 206 cal, 7 g prot, 184 mg sod, 41 g carb, 2 g fat, 0 mg chol, 44 mg calcium

- Preheat oven to 350°F. Lightly oil an 8" square baking dish.
- Combine first 8 ingredients in a medium-size bowl. Set aside.
- Blend tofu until smooth in food processor or mixing bowl. Blend in mashed banana and vanilla rice milk. Set aside.
- In a large bowl, whisk applesauce, FruitSource and vanilla. Add tofu mixture and blend until smooth.
- Add dry ingredients to liquid, mixing just until moistened. Fold in raisins and sunflower seeds.
- Spoon batter into prepared baking dish and sprinkle with nutmeg.
- Bake until golden brown and toothpick inserted in center comes out clean, about 30 minutes.

Hint:

Multi-blend flour is a high-protein blend made by milling a combination of whole grains and legumes. The Arrowhead Mills® brand is commonly available in natural food stores.

Nectarine Almond Spice Cake

Cinnamon, almonds and nectarines make this cake an excellent accompaniment for coffee or tea.

Total Time: 1 hour
Serves 12

1 cup whole wheat pastry flour
1/4 cup wheat germ
1 tsp. baking soda
1/2 tsp. baking powder
1 tsp. cinnamon
1/4 tsp. salt
1/2 cup unsweetened
   apple butter

1 cup brown sugar
1/4 cup lite silken tofu (extra firm)
1/2 cup rice milk or low-fat milk
1/2 tsp. almond extract
3 Tbsp. finely chopped almonds
3 cups unpeeled, sliced nectarines
1/2 cup Crunchy Cinnamon Oat
   Topping (recipe on page 91)

Per serving: 218 cal, 6 g prot, 161 mg sod, 47 g carb, 3 g fat, 0 mg chol, 43 mg calcium

Preheat oven to 350°F. Lightly oil an 8" square baking pan.
Combine first 6 ingredients in a medium-size bowl. Set aside.
Cream apple butter and brown sugar in a large bowl. Set aside.
Blend tofu until smooth in food processor or mixing bowl. Blend in rice milk and almond extract.
Whisk tofu mixture into creamed ingredients gradually.
Add dry ingredients to liquid ingredients and mix to form batter. Stir in almonds.
Arrange nectarines on bottom of pan. Pour batter over fruit. Sprinkle with topping.
Bake until toothpick inserted in center comes out clean, about 25 minutes. Cool in pan. Cut and serve.

Tangerine Dream Cake

Frost this luscious cake with Dreamy Tangerine Icing
(recipe on page 91) and serve it right out of the pan.

Total Time: 1 hour
Serves 16

2 cups whole wheat pastry flour
1 tsp. baking powder
1 tsp. cinnamon
2 tsp. baking soda
1/4 tsp. salt
2/3 cup Just Like Shortenin'™ (JLS)
1 1/2 cups brown sugar

2 Tbsp. egg replacer }
1/2 cup cold water }
* or 1/2 cup egg white*
1 tsp. vanilla extract
1/2 cup rice milk or low-fat milk
1 cup date nuggets or chopped dates
2 cups Dreamy Tangerine Icing
* (recipe on page 91)*

Per serving: 211 cal, 4 g prot, 194 mg sod, 49 g carb, 0.6 g fat, 0 mg chol, 66 mg calcium

- Preheat oven to 325°F. Lightly oil a 9" x 13" baking pan.
- Combine first 5 ingredients in a medium-size bowl. Set aside.
- Cream JLS and brown sugar in a large bowl.
- Whisk egg replacer with water until foamy and add to creamed ingredients. Stir vanilla.
- Add dry ingredients to liquid ingredients alternately with rice milk and mix to for batter. Fold in dates.
- Pour batter into pan and bake on middle rack of oven until toothpick inserted center comes out clean, about 25 minutes. Cool in pan. When completely cool, fre with icing.

Nothing warms the soul quite like homemade fruit crisps and cobblers. Cranberry Apple Crisp (recipe on page 42) and Spirited Peach Cobbler (recipe on page 51) make those chilly winter nights something to look forward to!

A chocolate lover's dream come true! Chocolate Dream Pie (recipe on page 40) is rich, creamy and delicious with **only 3 grams of fat** per serving.

Pies & Crusts

Brimming with glistening fruit or filled with creamy custard, pies can be just the treat to round out a meal. Twenty-minute no-bake pies are a staple around my house in the summer months. Simply blend walnuts, almonds and dates into a delicious No-Bake Pie Crust and fill it with the fresh fruits and flavorings of your choice.

Oven-baked pies and cobblers are equally simple to prepare. Their warm aromas wafting through the kitchen will chase the winter blues away. For a delightful finish to a holiday meal, serve Cranberry Apple Crisp, a tart and sweet cobbler topped with a cinnamon oat crust.

All of the recipes in this chapter are free of the refined sugar usually associated with pies. Instead, I use pure maple syrup or fruit sweeteners like FruitSource® and Mystic Lake®. I also use fruit juice concentrates in combination with Sucanat®, a granulated form of unrefined cane sugar that retains all of the vitamins and minerals provided by nature.

The custard cream pies in this chapter are free of eggs, butter and cream. This has significantly reduced the fat and calories without sacrificing taste or texture. Lite silken tofu creates a creamy custard filling in Blueberry Custard Pie, Mango Chiffon Pie and Classic Pumpkin Pie.

For an uncomplicated approach to a European classic, try the Easy Apple Strudel. Phyllo dough makes this a quick-to-assemble dessert that delivers exceptional flavor at half a gram of fat and 101 calories per serving. There are also several tasty crusts to choose from, including Cookie Crumb Crust, made with Health Valley® Fat-Free cookies, and a delicious Oat Bran Pie Crust with only 2 grams of fat per serving.

Whatever your choice, you will be delighted by the great taste and low-fat profile of these luscious pies and cobblers.

Banana Cream Pie

It's hard to believe this rich and creamy pie is dairy-free.

Total Time: 30 min.
Serves 8

1/2 cup frozen white grape juice
   concentrate
3 rounded Tbsp. agar flakes
2 (10.5 oz.) pkgs. lite silken tofu
   (extra firm)
2 medium-size ripe bananas
2 Tbsp. lemon juice

1 tsp. grated lemon rind
1/3 cup Mystic Lake® fruit sweetener
   or brown rice syrup
1 tsp. vanilla extract
1 (9") pre-baked Oat Bran
   Pie Crust (recipe on page 49)
1/8 tsp. nutmeg

Per serving: 229 cal, 10 g prot, 170 mg sod, 41 g carb, 3 g fat, 0 mg chol, 38 mg calcium

- Bring juice concentrate to a boil in a small saucepan. Sprinkle in agar and reduce heat to low. Simmer and stir until thickened, about 3 minutes. Remove from heat and set aside.
- Blend tofu until smooth in food processor or mixing bowl. Blend in bananas and thickened juice. Add lemon juice, lemon rind, sweetener and vanilla. Blend until smooth.
- Pour into pie crust and sprinkle with nutmeg. Refrigerate for 4 hours or overnight.

The Science of Soy

Recent research suggests that soybeans may be much more than just a rich source of plant protein. Certain substances found in soybeans prevent or slow the growth of cancer cells. Clinical studies have also shown that a diet using soy protein lowers cholesterol below levels reached by traditional low-fat, low cholesterol diets. *

*U.S. News and World Report, May 31, 1993

Blueberry Custard Pie

Enjoy the rich taste and texture of this delectable custard pie.

**Total Time: 40 min.
Serves 8**

2 cups vanilla rice milk or
 low-fat milk
1/3 cup liquid FruitSource®
 or brown rice syrup
2 rounded Tbsp. agar flakes
1 (10.5 oz.) pkg. lite silken tofu
 (extra firm)

1 tsp. vanilla extract
1/4 tsp. cinnamon
1/8 tsp. nutmeg
1 (9") pre-baked Oat Bran Pie Crust
 (recipe on page 49)
3 cups Blueberry Topping (recipe on
 page 86)

Per serving: 229 cal, 8 g prot, 139 mg sod, 44 g carb, 3 g fat, 0 mg chol, 18 mg calcium

- Bring rice milk and FruitSource to a boil in a medium-size saucepan. Sprinkle in agar and reduce heat to low. Simmer and stir until thickened, about 3 minutes. Remove from heat and set aside.
- Blend tofu until smooth in food processor or mixing bowl. Blend in vanilla, cinnamon and nutmeg.
- Whisk tofu mixture into thickened rice milk, 1/3 at a time. When smooth, return mixture to a boil, stirring constantly. Set aside to cool for at least 15 minutes.

To assemble:
- Pour cooled filling into pre-baked pie crust.* Spoon topping evenly over filling and refrigerate for at least one hour.

Hint:

**You can make this pie
ahead by refrigerating
the filled crust. Then,
prepare Blueberry
Topping up to 1/2 hour
before serving.*

Chocolate Dream Pie

This incredibly creamy chocolate pie has a pudding-like consistency and a rich chocolate flavor.

Total Time: 30 min.
Serves 10

2 (10.5 oz.) pkgs. lite silken tofu
  (extra firm)
1/2 cup cocoa powder
3/4 cup liquid FruitSource® or
  brown rice syrup

3 tsp. vanilla extract
1 (9") pre-baked Oat Bran Pie
  Crust (recipe on page 49)

Per serving: 198 cal, 9 g prot, 126 mg sod, 34 g carb, 3 g fat, 0 mg chol, 36 mg calcium

- Blend tofu until smooth in food processor or mixing bowl. Set aside.
- Place cocoa in a small bowl. Set aside.
- Heat FruitSource for 90 seconds in microwave or 3 minutes over low heat.
- Pour over cocoa and whisk until smooth.
- Pour cocoa syrup and vanilla into tofu and blend until smooth.
- Pour into pie crust and refrigerate for 4 hours or overnight. Serve chilled.

Hint:

For Rich 'N Creamy Chocolate Pudding, serve this filling in dessert cups without the crust. Garnish with sliced fresh bananas and strawberries.

Food of the Gods

The Aztecs called cocoa "food of the gods" and drinking chocolate was a feature of Spanish cuisine in the seventeenth century. Today, it is estimated that over one million tons of cocoa products are consumed every year.

Classic Pumpkin Pie

As rich and delectable as the original—without the calories and cholesterol!

Total Time: 1 hour
Serves 8

2 (10.5 oz.) pkgs. lite silken tofu
  (extra firm)
1 (16 oz.) can pumpkin purée
3/4 cup Sucanat® or brown sugar
2 tsp. cinnamon
1/2 tsp. nutmeg

1/2 tsp. ground ginger
1/4 tsp. ground cloves
1/8 tsp. salt
1 (9") Oat Bran Pie Crust
  (recipe on page 49)

Per serving: 207 cal, 10 g prot, 205 mg sod, 37 g carb, 3 g fat, 0 mg chol, 62 mg calcium

- Preheat oven to 375°F.
- Blend tofu until smooth in food processor or mixing bowl. Blend in remaining ingredients.
- Spoon into pie crust and bake on center rack of oven for 45 minutes. Serve warm or refrigerate until serving time.

Cookie Crumb Crust

This quick and easy no-bake pie crust complements any chilled filling.

Total Time: 1 hour
Makes one 9" pie crust

1 (6 1/4 oz.) pkg. Health Valley®
  Fat-Free cookies
1/2 cup wheat germ

1/4 cup dark raisins
1/4 cup frozen apple juice
  concentrate

Per serving (one pie slice): 133 cal, 6 g prot, 64 mg sod, 25 g carb, 2 g fat, 0 mg chol, 28 mg calcium

- Blend cookies until crumbly in a food processor or blender. Blend in wheat germ and raisins.
- Blend in juice concentrate until dough forms. Mixture will seem wet. Do not adjust.
- Press into a 9" pie plate with dampened fingers and refrigerate until ready to fill.

Cranberry Apple Crisp

A delicious layered cobbler, topped with a crunchy cinnamon topping.

Total Time: 1 hour
Serves 8

5 cups cored, peeled and
    sliced apples
2 Tbsp. lemon juice
1 cup frozen apple juice
    concentrate
1 cup Sucanat® or brown sugar
1 tsp. cinnamon

2 Tbsp. cornstarch
2 Tbsp. cold water
1 (12 oz.) pkg. frozen cranberries or
    3 cups fresh
1/2 tsp. almond extract
2 cups Cinnamon Cobbler Topping
    (recipe on page 88)

Per serving: 263 cal, 5 g prot, 60 mg sod, 58 g carb, 3 g fat, 0 mg chol, 50 mg calcium

- Preheat oven to 350°F. Lightly oil a 2-quart baking dish.
- Toss apples with lemon juice in a large saucepan.
- Add 1/2 cup of juice concentrate and cook over medium heat until thawed, about 3 minutes.
- Stir in 1/4 cup of Sucanat and cinnamon. Reduce heat to low and simmer, stirring frequently, until apples are softened, about 8 to 10 minutes.
- Dissolve cornstarch in water and add to apple mixture. Simmer until thickened, about 5 minutes. Remove from heat and set aside.
- Heat remaining juice concentrate and cranberries in a medium-size saucepan over medium heat until berries begin to pop, about 5 minutes. Add remaining Sucanat and almond extract.
- Simmer until thickened, about 5 minutes. You will not need any thickening agent, since cranberries will thicken on their own.
- Spoon apple mixture across bottom of prepared baking dish. Spoon cranberry mixture over apples and sprinkle with topping.
- Bake until topping is golden brown and filling bubbles through, about 30 minutes. Spoon into dessert dishes. Serve warm.

Hint:

For quick assembly, prepare the apple and cranberry fillings simultaneously in separate saucepans.

Easy Apple Strudel

Impress your guests with this no-fuss version a classic dessert.

Total Time: 1 hour
Serves 16

4 cups cored, peeled and chopped
  Granny Smith apples
2 Tbsp. lemon juice
1 1/2 cups Sucanat® or
  brown sugar
1/2 cup golden raisins

2 tsp. cinnamon
1/2 tsp. nutmeg
1/2 cup fine bread crumbs
6 sheets phyllo dough*
Canola oil cooking spray

Per serving: 101 cal, 2 g prot, 85 mg sod, 24 g carb, 0.5 g fat, 0 mg chol, 16 mg calcium

- Preheat oven to 375°F. Lightly oil cookie sheet.
- Toss apples with lemon juice and Sucanat. Stir in raisins, one teaspoon cinnamon and nutmeg. Set aside.
- Combine bread crumbs and remaining cinnamon in a small bowl. Set aside.
- Thaw phyllo dough (see "Techniques" on page 10).
- Gently remove phyllo sheets from package. Wrap remainder tightly in plastic and return to refrigerator or freezer.
- Place the dough on a sheet of wax paper and cover with a damp kitchen towel.
- Keep a water mister handy to spray the towel, keeping it damp.

To assemble: *(See illustrations on page 44.)*
- Place two 20" pieces of wax paper side by side on the work surface lengthwise, overlapping slightly along the center.
- Gently remove one sheet of phyllo and center it on the wax paper work surface. Spray phyllo with canola oil and sprinkle with 1 1/2 tablespoons cinnamon bread crumbs.
- Place a second sheet of phyllo over the first sheet. Spray second sheet with canola oil and sprinkle with 1 1/2 tablespoons cinnamon bread crumbs. Repeat this layering process with remaining phyllo and bread crumbs. Use all remaining bread crumbs before the top sheet is in place. Spray top sheet.
- Spoon apple filling in a 4-inch-wide column 4 inches from one of the short sides of the rectangular dough. (If filling is very liquid, drain slightly with a slotted spoon before placing onto dough.)

- Lift the wax paper to fold the short side of dough over filling. Continue to lift the wax paper to roll up the dough and filling, jelly-roll style, into a tight strudel.
- Place cookie sheet next to work surface. Slide folded strudel, seam side down, onto prepared cookie sheet. Fold ends under to seal.
- Bake on upper rack of oven until crisp and golden brown, about 20 minutes. Cool slightly, cut and serve.

Hints:

See "Techniques" on page 10 for tips on using phyllo dough. If you prefer not to use cooking spray, brush phyllo lightly with canola oil.

Folding instructions for Easy Apple Strudel

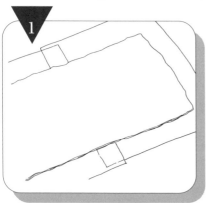 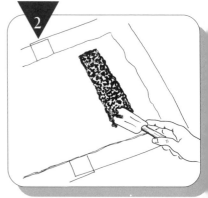

1) Place wax paper on work surface. Center one sheet of dough on wax paper and mist with cooking oil spray. Sprinkle with bread crumbs. Repeat with remaining dough and bread crumbs. Mist top sheet of dough. 2) Spoon filling in a 4-inch-wide column 4 inches from one of the short sides of dough.

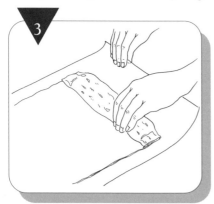 

3) Lift wax paper to fold short side of dough over filling. Continue to lift wax paper and roll up filled dough into a tight strudel. 4) Slide folded strudel, seam-side down, onto cookie sheet. Fold ends under to seal.

Easy Mini-Strudels

Makes 4

- Proceed as directed for large strudel on page 43, except use 12 sheets of phyllo. Using 6 sheets of phyllo and one 20" sheet of wax paper at a time, layer dough with cinnamon bread crumbs as directed to the point of arranging the apple filling. *(See figure 1.)* Reserve remaining 6 sheets of phyllo.
- Before filling, use kitchen shears to cut the dough in half horizontally, right through the wax paper. You should now have two long pieces of dough. *(See figure 2.)*
- Spoon 1 1/2 cups of filling in a 4-inch-wide column 4 inches from end of each piece of dough. Roll up as directed. *(See figure 3.)*
- Place each mini-strudel seam side down on prepared cookie sheet. Fold ends under to seal. *(See figure 4.)*
- Repeat with remaining 6 sheets of phyllo.
- Bake until crisp and golden brown, about 15 minutes.

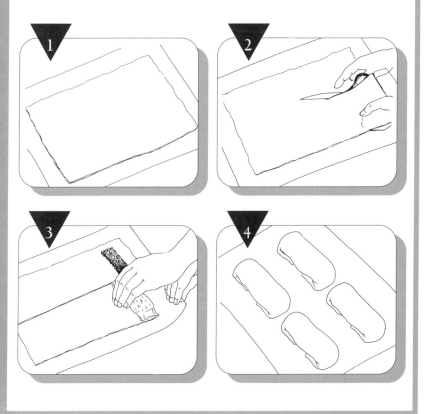

Mango Chiffon Pie

*Golden mangoes give this pie a beautiful color
and a delicate, creamy flavor.*

**Total Time: 20 min.
Serves 8**

1/2 cup frozen apple juice
   concentrate
3 rounded Tbsp. agar flakes
1 (16 oz.) pkg. frozen mango
   chunks
1 (10.5 oz.) pkg. lite silken tofu
   (extra firm)

1 medium-size banana, mashed
1 Tbsp. lemon juice
1/2 cup Mystic Lake® fruit sweetener
   or brown rice syrup
1 (9") Cookie Crumb Crust
   (recipe on page 41)
1 Tbsp. shredded coconut

Per serving: 309 cal, 10 g prot, 122 mg sod, 66 g carb, 3 g fat, 0 mg chol, 57 mg calcium

- Bring juice concentrate to a boil in a small saucepan. Sprinkle in agar and reduce heat to low. Simmer and stir until thickened, about 3 minutes.
- Add mango and simmer, stirring frequently, for 10 minutes. Remove from heat and set aside.
- Blend tofu until smooth in food processor or mixing bowl. Blend in banana, lemon juice and sweetener. Add mango mixture and blend until smooth.
- Return mixture to saucepan and bring to a boil. Reduce heat to low and simmer, stirring constantly for 5 minutes.
- Pour into crust and sprinkle with coconut.
- Refrigerate for 4 hours or overnight.

Hint:

For more tropical flavor, use Health Valley® Hawaiian Fruit cookies in the Cookie Crumb Crust (recipe on page 41).

No-Bake Peach Pie

Sweet, ripe peaches make a wonderful no-bake filling.

Total Time: 10 min.
Serves 10

4 to 6 cups peeled,
  sliced peaches
1 Tbsp. pure maple syrup

1/4 tsp. almond extract
1 (9") No-Bake Pie Crust
  (recipe below)

Per serving: 140 cal, 2 g prot, 22 mg sod, 28 g carb, 4 g fat, 0 mg chol, 23 mg calcium

- Toss fruit with maple syrup and almond extract in a large bowl.
- Arrange fruit in pie crust and refrigerate until serving time.

Hint:

For a more colorful pie, try a filling of mixed fruit such as peaches and strawberries.

No-Bake Pie Crust

*This basic no-bake crust is a snap to make
and will enhance any chilled pie filling.*

Total Time: 5 min.
Makes one 9" pie crust

1/4 cup almonds
1/4 cup walnuts
1 1/2 cups soft dates

Per serving (one pie slice): 112 cal, 2 g prot, 21 mg sod, 21 g carb, 4 g fat, 0 mg chol, 20 mg calcium

Grind almonds and walnuts in a food processor or blender. Remove to a small bowl and set aside.
Place dates in food processor or blender and blend to a paste. Add ground nuts and blend until smooth.
Turn into pie plate. Press to fill plate and form crust.
Fill with your favorite no-bake filling, refrigerate and enjoy!

No-Bake Strawberry Pie

So luscious and so incredibly simple,
you'll want to make this a summer standard.

Total Time: 1 hour
Serves 16

4 cups fresh, ripe strawberries
1 Tbsp. pure maple syrup
1 (9") No-Bake Pie Crust (previous recipe)

Per serving: 135 cal, 2 g prot, 22 mg sod, 27 g carb, 4 g fat, 0 mg chol, 28 mg calcium

- Rinse, drain and pat dry strawberries. Slice and place in a medium-size bowl.
- Toss strawberries with maple syrup. Use only one tablespoon of syrup per quart strawberries, as sweeteners increase the moisture of the fruit.
- Arrange strawberries in pie crust. Refrigerate until serving time.

Garden Fresh

I first tried a pie like this one in a tiny restaurant in Ventura, California called Garden Fresh. They offered a menu which featured only raw ingredients. The food was good, but the pies were great. Enjoy!

No-Bake Tips

When making no-bake fillings, keep in mind that the sweetener draws the juices out of the fruit. So make the filling no more than one hour before serving. If the fruit is very ripe and juicy, drain it in a colander before adding the sweetener.

Oat Bran Pie Crust

*This is my favorite pie crust. It's an especially good crust
for creamy, custard-like fillings.*

**Total Time: 20 min.
Makes one 9" crust**

1/4 cup lite silken tofu
  (extra firm)
1 3/4 cups whole wheat
  pastry flour
1/4 cup oat bran

1/4 tsp. salt
2 rounded Tbsp. liquid Fruit Source®
  or brown rice syrup
1 Tbsp. canola oil
1/4 cup ice water

Per serving (one pie slice): 126 cal, 5 g prot, 64 mg sod, 23 g carb, 2 g fat, 0 mg chol, 13 mg calcium

Lightly oil a 9" pie pan.
Blend tofu until smooth in food processor or mixing bowl. Blend in flour, oat bran
and salt. Blend in FruitSource and oil until crumbly, about one minute. Blend in
water until dough forms a ball.
Turn dough onto lightly floured wax paper and top with second sheet. Flatten into
disc and roll into a circle 1/8" to 1/4" thick.
Peel off top sheet of wax paper and lay dough over pie pan. Peel off second sheet and
gently press dough into pan. Trim and shape around edges.

Pre-baked Pie Crust

- *Preheat oven to 400°F. Prick dough with a fork and place raw dry beans on top
  to prevent dough from bubbling. Place pie plate on a cookie sheet in center rack
  of oven and bake until lightly browned, about 15 minutes.*

To Bake Pie Crust With Filling

- *Refrigerate pressed, trimmed, unbaked pie crust until filling is prepared. Proceed
  with desired recipe.*

Soft-Crust Apple Pie

*Cinnamon, nutmeg and cardamom will entice you
to sample a piece of this easy apple pie.*

Total Time: 1 hour
Serves 16

6 to 7 cups cored, peeled and sliced
  apples
1 cup Sucanat® or brown sugar
1 Tbsp. cornstarch
1 tsp. cinnamon
1/2 tsp. nutmeg
1 cup rolled oats
1 cup unbleached all-purpose flour

1/4 cup wheat germ
1 cup granulated FruitSource®
  or brown sugar
1 tsp. ground cardamom
1/2 cup lite silken tofu (extra firm)
1/4 cup rice milk or low-fat milk
1 tsp. vanilla extract
1/3 cup Just Like Shortenin'™ (JLS)

Per serving: 223 cal, 5 g prot, 29 mg sod, 49 g carb, 2 g fat, 0 mg chol, 21 mg calcium

- Preheat oven to 350°F. Lightly oil a 9" x 13" baking pan.
- Toss apple slices with Sucanat, cornstarch, cinnamon and nutmeg. Set aside.
- Combine next 5 ingredients in food processor or mixing bowl, using pulse technique. Remove to a medium-size bowl.
- Blend tofu until smooth in food processor or mixing bowl. Blend in rice milk and vanilla. Add JLS and process until smooth.
- Add dry ingredients to tofu mixture gradually, using pulse technique until dough forms a ball.
- Press dough into pan to form crust. Arrange apples over crust, cover with foil and bake for 20 minutes.
- Remove foil and bake until apples are tender, about 15 minutes.
- Cool slightly in pan. Serve warm or chilled.

Spirited Peach Cobbler

This down-home, deep dish fruit pie is traditionally served warm.

Total Time: 45 min.
Serves 8

1 cup frozen white grape juice concentrate
2 (16 oz.) pkgs. frozen sliced peaches (about 6 cups)
1/3 cup Sucanat® or brown sugar

1/4 cup peach brandy
2 Tbsp. cornstarch
2 Tbsp. cold water
1 1/2 cups Cinnamon Cobbler Topping (recipe on page 88)

Per serving: 206 cal, 49 g prot, 30 mg sod, 41 g carb, 2 g fat, 0 mg chol, 31 mg calcium

Preheat oven to 350°F.

In a stove-top safe, ovenproof 2-quart casserole dish, heat juice concentrate over medium heat until thawed. Add peaches, reduce heat and simmer until peaches are just thawed, about 3 minutes.

Stir in Sucanat and brandy and simmer until mixture becomes syrupy, about 3 minutes.

Remove 1 1/2 cups of syrup to a small saucepan and set aside.

Dissolve cornstarch in water and stir into peach mixture until thickened.

Sprinkle with topping and bake until lightly browned and filling bubbles through, about 30 minutes.

Bring reserved syrup to a boil over medium heat, stirring frequently to reduce syrup to 1 cup, about 10 minutes.

Spoon over warm cobbler and serve.

Whole Wheat Pie Crust

Flavorful whole grains make this a cholesterol-free crust you'll want to use often.

Total Time: 20 min.
Makes one 9" pie crust

1 cup plus 6 Tbsp. whole wheat
   pastry flour
2 Tbsp. wheat germ

1/8 tsp. salt
2 Tbsp. canola oil
1/4 cup ice water

Per serving (one pie slice): 88 cal, 3 g prot, 30 mg sod, 16 g carb, 3 g fat, 0 mg chol, 9 mg calcium

- Combine flour, wheat germ and salt in food processor or mixing bowl. Blend in oil until crumbly, about one minute. Blend in ice water until dough forms a ball.
- Turn dough onto lightly floured wax paper and top with second sheet. Flatten into disc and roll into a circle 1/8" to 1/4" thick.
- Peel off top sheet of wax paper and lay dough over pie pan. Peel off second sheet and gently press dough into pan. Trim and shape around edges.

Hint:

For tips on pre-baked and unbaked pie crusts, see page 49.

Whole Grain Flours

Use organically grown, whole grain, stone ground flours whenever possible. These flours retain their essential nutrients because the bran is intact.

*Chocolate Bon Bons (recipe on page 60) and Raspberry Apricot Oat Bars (recipe on page 70) make delicious snacks for the lunchbox—or anytime. Each delectable treat has **only 3 grams of fat!***

Go ahead—have a brownie! Decadently rich Fudgy Chocolate Brownies (recipe on page 66) clock in at **just 0.3 grams of fat** per brownie. Or try Creamy Peanut Butter DeLites (recipe on page 65), bursting with the natural flavor of peanut butter and **only 1 gram of fat** per cookie.

Cookies & Bars

Cookies are a universal treat. They make excellent lunchbox stuffers, holiday fare or anytime snacks. The guiltless goodies in this chapter include some light and luscious, some rich and chocolatey, and some chewy and chock full of fruit and nuts. Yes, nuts! The basic ingredients in these recipes are so incredibly low in fat, there's actually room for a little nutty indulgence.

Cookies are traditionally laden with fat and calories, due to the butter and eggs used. But you'll find none of that here. Without sacrificing flavor or texture, these delightful confections use low-fat ingredients like natural applesauce and prune butter (a fruit purée) found in your local supermarket. Just Like Shortenin'™ (JLS) is a new product that works wonders in recipes like Raspberry Apricot Oat Bars, a delicious bar cookie with a chewy raspberry filling and a crunchy oat crust.

If you're looking for chocolate, you've reached the right chapter. Nearly half of the recipes here are bursting with fudgy chocolate flavor, and none has more than 4 grams of fat per serving. Just try to resist the Chocolate Bon Bons or the Chocolate Truffles. Each Chocolate Truffle has only 2 grams of fat and you can make dozens of them in only 20 minutes! What could be better!? Only one thing could top that—a Fudgy Chocolate Brownie loaded with gooey chocolate flavor and only 0.3 grams of fat. Try 'em!

Awesome Peach Dessert Bars

Filled with moist, brandied peaches and topped with Luscious Carob Icing (recipe on page 93), these dessert bars will make you swoon.

Total Time: 1 hour
Makes 32 bars

1/2 cup peach brandy
1 1/2 cups dried peaches, chopped
2 Tbsp. lemon juice ⎱
1 cup soy milk lite ⎰
    or 1 cup buttermilk
2 cups unbleached all-purpose flour
1 tsp. baking soda
1 tsp. baking powder
1 1/4 cups Sucanat® or brown sugar

1/2 tsp. cinnamon
1/2 tsp. ground cardamom
1/2 cup natural applesauce
2 Tbsp. egg replacer ⎱
1/2 cup cold water ⎰
    or 1/2 cup egg white
3 cups Luscious Carob Icing
    (recipe on page 93)

Per bar: 125 cal, 2 g prot, 71 mg sod, 27 g carb, 0.2 g fat, 0 mg chol, 37 mg calcium

- Preheat oven to 350°F. Lightly oil a jelly roll pan.
- Bring brandy and peaches to a boil in a small saucepan.
- Reduce heat to low and simmer until brandy is almost absorbed, about 5 minutes. Remove from heat and set aside.
- Add lemon juice to soy milk and set aside.
- Combine next 6 ingredients in a medium-size bowl. Set aside.
- Measure applesauce into a large bowl.
- Whisk egg replacer with water until foamy and add to applesauce. Whisk in soy "buttermilk" mixture and blend until smooth.
- Add dry ingredients to liquid ingredients and mix to form batter. Fold in brandied peaches.
- Pour into pan and bake until toothpick inserted in center comes out clean, about 25 minutes. Cool in pan. When completely cool, frost with icing.

Banana Date DeLites

Soft, fragrant and delightful!

Total Time: 30 min.
Makes about 4 1/2 dozen

1 cup whole wheat pastry flour
1 1/2 cups rolled oats
1 tsp. baking soda
1 tsp. cinnamon
1/8 tsp. nutmeg
3/4 cup natural applesauce
1/2 cup liquid FruitSource® or
  brown rice syrup

2 Tbsp. egg replacer }
1/2 cup cold water }
  or 1/2 cup egg white
1 tsp. vanilla extract
1 medium-size ripe
  banana, mashed
1/2 cup date nuggets or
  chopped dates

Per cookie: 45 cal, 1 g prot, 16 mg sod, 9 g carb, 0.5 g fat, 0 mg chol, 4 mg calcium

- Preheat oven to 375°F. Lightly oil cookie sheets.
- Combine first 5 ingredients in a medium-size bowl. Set aside.
- Blend applesauce and FruitSource in a large bowl.
- Whisk egg replacer with water until foamy and add to applesauce mixture. Blend in vanilla, banana and dates.
- Add dry ingredients to liquid ingredients and mix to form batter.
- Drop by rounded teaspoonfuls onto cookie sheets.
- Bake 10 to 12 minutes. Cool on sheets for 5 minutes and remove to wire racks to cool completely.

Inspirational Applesauce

My introduction to the idea of using fruit purées as a fat replacer came from an ad for Mott's applesauce. Mott's U.S.A. was a pioneer in researching baking without added fats.

Carrot Cookie Bars

*Frost these light and cake-like cookie bars with Pineapple
Supreme Icing (recipe on page 94).*

Total Time: 1 hour
Makes 24 bars

1 (8 oz.) can crushed pineapple
   packed in juice
2 Tbsp. lemon juice ⎱
1 cup soy milk lite ⎰
   or 1 cup buttermilk
1 cup rolled oats
1 cup whole wheat pastry flour
1 tsp. baking soda
1 tsp. baking powder
1 tsp. cinnamon

1/2 tsp. nutmeg
1/2 cup prune butter
1 cup brown sugar
2 Tbsp. egg replacer ⎱
1/2 cup cold water ⎰
   or 1/2 cup egg white
1 tsp. grated lemon rind
2 cups grated carrots
3 cups Pineapple Supreme Icing
   (recipe on page 94)

Per bar: 129 cal, 4 g prot, 79 mg sod, 28 g carb, 1 g fat, 0 mg chol, 36 mg calcium

- Preheat oven to 350°F. Lightly oil a 9" x 13" baking pan.
- Drain pineapple, reserving juice for icing. Set aside.
- Add lemon juice to soy milk and set aside.
- Grind oats into oat flour in food processor or blender. Remove to a medium-size bowl and stir in next 5 ingredients. Set aside.
- Cream prune butter and brown sugar in a large bowl.
- Whisk egg replacer with water until foamy and add to creamed ingredients. Blend in lemon rind and soy "buttermilk" mixture.
- Add dry ingredients to liquid ingredients and mix to form batter. Fold in pineapple and carrots.
- Pour into pan and bake until toothpick inserted in center comes out clean, about 30 minutes. Cool in pan. When completely cool, frost with icing.

Chock Full of Fruit & Nut Bars

Tart cranberries, crunchy walnuts and sweet golden raisins make this an outstanding cookie bar.

Total Time: 1 hour
Makes 24 bars

1 cup rolled oats
1 cup soy milk lite or
   low-fat milk
1 cup unbleached
   all-purpose flour
1 tsp. baking soda
1 tsp. baking powder
1/2 tsp. cinnamon
1/4 tsp. nutmeg
1/4 tsp. salt
1/2 cup brown sugar

1/4 cup natural applesauce
2 Tbsp. egg replacer
1/2 cup cold water }
   or 1/2 cup egg white
1 tsp. vanilla extract
1/2 cup dried cranberries or
   dried cherries
1/4 cup golden raisins
1/4 cup chopped walnuts or
   chopped cashews
1/4 tsp. cinnamon

Per bar: 89 cal, 3 g prot, 82 mg sod, 17 g carb, 2 g fat, 0 mg chol, 24 mg calcium

- Preheat oven to 350°F. Lightly oil a 9" x 13" baking pan.
- Combine oats and soy milk in a large bowl. Set aside.
- Sift next 6 ingredients into a medium-size bowl. Stir in brown sugar and set aside.
- Add applesauce to oat mixture.
- Whisk egg replacer with water until foamy and add to oat mixture. Stir in vanilla.
- Add dry ingredients to liquid ingredients and mix to form batter. Fold in cranberries, raisins and walnuts.
- Pour into pan and sprinkle with cinnamon. Bake until golden brown, about 30 minutes. Cool in pan. Cut and serve.

Chocolate Bon Bons

These easy-to-make marvels are a 4-star treat.
I could never make them too often!

Total Time: 45 min.
Makes about 3 1/2 dozen

1 (7 1/2 oz.) pkg. amaranth
    graham crackers
1 cup dark raisins
1/2 cup cashew pieces
1/2 cup peanut butter
2 Tbsp. soy milk lite or
    low-fat milk

1/2 tsp. vanilla extract
3 Tbsp. pure maple syrup
2 Tbsp. egg replacer ⎫
1/2 cup cold water ⎭
    or 1/2 cup egg white

Coating:
1 cup Sunspire® semisweet
    chocolate chips
2 Tbsp. Mystic Lake® fruit
    sweetener or brown rice syrup

2 Tbsp. Sucanat® or
    brown sugar
1 tsp. vanilla extract
2 Tbsp. water

Per cookie: 74 cal, 1 g prot, 37 mg sod, 12 g carb, 3 g fat, 0 mg chol, 31 mg calcium

- Line a cookie sheet with wax paper. Lightly oil paper.
- Grind graham crackers into crumbs in food processor or blender.
- Blend in raisins and cashews. Blend in next 4 ingredients.
- Whisk egg replacer and water until foamy. Add to graham cracker mixture and blend
- Roll mixture into 1" balls. Place on cookie sheet and set aside.

To make coating:
- Melt chocolate chips in a double boiler, about 3 minutes. Add remaining ingredients
  Cook and stir until smooth, about 10 minutes. Remove from heat.
- Dip balls into chocolate. Remove coated balls using 2 spoons to drain excess coating
  Return to cookie sheet and refrigerate for at least 20 minutes. Serve.

Chocolate Chip Cookie Bars

*Chunks of chocolate, chewy raisins and hearty
oatmeal will satisfy any sweet tooth!*

**Total Time: 1 hour
Makes 24 bars**

2 Tbsp. lemon juice ⎫
1 cup soy milk lite ⎭
   or 1 cup buttermilk
1 2/3 cups unbleached
   all-purpose flour
1 tsp. baking soda
1 tsp. baking powder
1 tsp. cinnamon
1/4 tsp. salt
1/2 cup natural applesauce

2 cups brown sugar
2 Tbsp. egg replacer ⎫
1/2 cup cold water ⎭
   or 1/2 cup egg white
2 tsp. vanilla extract
3 cups rolled oats
1 cup Sunspire® semisweet
   chocolate chips
1 cup dark raisins

Per bar: 263 cal, 7 g prot, 91 mg sod, 54 g carb, 4 g fat, 0 mg chol, 81 mg calcium

- Preheat oven to 375°F. Lightly oil a 9" x 13" baking pan.
- Add lemon juice to soy milk and set aside.
- Combine next 5 ingredients in a medium-size bowl. Set aside.
- Mix applesauce and brown sugar in a large bowl.
- Whisk egg replacer with water until foamy and add to applesauce mixture. Blend in vanilla and soy "buttermilk" mixture.
- Add dry ingredients to liquid ingredients and mix to form batter. Fold in oats, chocolate chips and raisins.
- Pour into pan and bake until toothpick inserted in center comes out clean, about 30 minutes. Cool in pan. Cut and serve.

Chocolate Fruit Treasures

*These rich dark chocolate treats will store refrigerated
for up to a week and frozen for up to a month.*

**Total Time: 20 min.
Makes 2 1/2 dozen**

1 cup Sunspire® dark
   chocolate chips
2 Tbsp. Mystic Lake® fruit
   sweetener or brown rice syrup
2 Tbsp. Sucanat® or
   brown sugar
1 tsp. vanilla extract

2 Tbsp. water
1 cup chopped dried pears
1/2 cup date pieces or
   chopped dates
1/2 cup golden raisins
1/4 cup chopped almonds

Per cookie: 63 cal, 0.6 g prot, 13 mg sod, 13 g carb, 2 g fat, 0 mg chol, 33 mg calcium

- Line cookie sheets with wax paper. Lightly oil paper.
- Melt chocolate chips in a double boiler, about 3 minutes. Add next 4 ingredients Cook and stir until smooth, about 10 minutes.
- Stir in remaining ingredients, mixing thoroughly. Remove from heat and cool slightly.
- Drop by rounded tablespoonfuls onto cookie sheets and refrigerate for at least 20 minutes.

Hint:

*Store in the freezer
for a more firm,
chewy treat.*

Chocolate Fudge Oaties

These delectable treats can be eaten right out of the freezer.
Instead of freezing, they form a chewy, fudgy center.

Total Time: 20 min.
Makes 2 dozen

1/2 cup liquid FruitSource® or brown rice syrup	3/4 cup soy milk lite or low-fat milk
1/4 cup prune butter	2 1/2 cups rolled oats
1/4 cup peanut butter	1 tsp. cinnamon
1/2 cup Sucanat® or brown sugar	1/2 tsp. almond extract
1/4 cup cocoa powder	1/2 cup golden raisins
	1/3 cup finely chopped almonds

Per bar: 157 cal, 6 g prot, 32 mg sod, 27 g carb, 4 g fat, 0 mg chol, 13 mg calcium

- Oil a 9" x 13" pan. Line with wax paper and lightly oil paper.
- Combine FruitSource, prune butter and peanut butter in a large saucepan over medium heat. Simmer for 2 minutes, stirring constantly.
- Stir in Sucanat and cocoa until blended, about 2 minutes. Remove from heat and stir in soy milk.
- Add oats and mix thoroughly. Stir in cinnamon and almond extract. Fold in raisins and almonds.
- Spread mixture into pan and freeze for 4 hours or overnight. Cut and serve.

Notes on Oats

Oats contain natural antioxidants which boost your immunity.
These antioxidants also extend the keeping quality of any food to
which oats are added.

Chocolate Truffles

These rich and creamy no-bake wonders have only 2 grams of fat!

Total Time: 30 min.
   Makes 3 dozen

1 cup dried apricots,
   cut into strips
2 cups golden raisins
1/2 cup Mandarine Napoleon®
   liqueur or Grand Marnier®
1 (10.5 oz.) pkg. lite silken tofu
   (extra firm)

1/2 cup pure maple syrup
1/4 cup cocoa powder
1/3 cup frozen white grape
   juice concentrate
3 rounded Tbsp. agar flakes

Coating:
1 cup Sunspire® dark
   chocolate chips
2 Tbsp. water

2 Tbsp. pure maple syrup
1 tsp. vanilla extract
2 Tbsp. Sucanat® or brown sugar

Per cookie: 111 cal, 2 g prot, 16 mg sod, 23 g carb, 2 g fat, 0 mg chol, 35 mg calcium

- Line cookie sheets with wax paper. Lightly oil paper.
- Combine apricots, raisins and liqueur in a medium-size saucepan over low heat. Simmer until liqueur has almost been absorbed, about 10 minutes. Set aside.
- Blend tofu until smooth in food processor or mixing bowl. Blend in maple syrup and cocoa. Set aside.
- Bring juice concentrate to a boil in a small saucepan. Sprinkle in agar and reduce heat to low. Simmer and stir until thickened, about 3 minutes.
- Pour thickened juice into tofu mixture and blend thoroughly. Add tofu mixture to fruit mixture and simmer over low heat, stirring constantly, for 5 minutes.
- Drop by rounded tablespoonfuls onto cookie sheets.

To make coating:
- Melt chocolate chips in a double boiler, about 3 minutes. Add remaining ingredients and cook and stir until smooth, about 10 minutes.
- Dip balls of truffle mixture into coating. Remove each truffle with 2 spoons to drain excess coating.
- Return to cookie sheets and refrigerate for 20 minutes. Remove to an airtight container, placing oiled wax paper between layers. Cover and freeze until ready to serve.

Hint:

These delicious truffles won't freeze. Instead, they will form a chewy center Serve them right out of the freezer!

Creamy Peanut Butter DeLites

You won't believe these light and creamy peanut butter cookies contain no sugar and no cholesterol.

Total Time: 40 min.
Makes about 3 1/2 dozen

1 cup whole wheat pastry flour
1/4 cup wheat germ
1 1/2 tsp. baking soda
1/2 tsp. baking powder
1/2 tsp. cinnamon
1/2 cup prune butter
1/2 cup natural peanut butter

3 Tbsp. liquid FruitSource®
  or brown rice syrup
2 Tbsp. egg replacer }
1/2 cup cold water }
  or 1/2 cup egg white
1/4 cup soy milk lite or
  low-fat milk
1 tsp. vanilla extract

Per serving (2 cookies): 33 cal, 1 g prot, 36 mg sod, 4 g carb, 1 g fat, 0 mg chol, 7 mg calcium

- Preheat oven to 375°F. Lightly oil cookie sheets.
- Combine first 5 ingredients in a medium-size bowl.
- Cream prune butter and peanut butter in a large bowl. Blend in FruitSource until smooth.
- Whisk egg replacer with water until foamy and add to creamed ingredients. Blend in soy milk and vanilla until smooth.
- Add dry ingredients to liquid ingredients and mix to form batter.
- Drop by rounded tablespoonfuls onto cookie sheets.
- Bake 5 to 8 minutes. Cool on sheets for 5 minutes and remove to wire racks to cool completely.

Fudgy Chocolate Brownies

I haven't found a more delicious, fudgy, satisfying brownie—
with or without the walnuts!

Total Time: 45 min.
Makes 12 brownies

2 Tbsp. lemon juice ⎫
1 cup soy milk lite ⎭
  or 1 cup buttermilk
1 cup unbleached
  all-purpose flour
1 tsp. baking soda
1 tsp. baking powder
1 cup cocoa powder

1/4 tsp. salt
1 cup prune butter
2 cups brown sugar
2 Tbsp. egg replacer ⎫
1/2 cup cold water   ⎭
  or 1/2 cup egg white
1 tsp. vanilla extract
1/4 cup chopped walnuts (optional)

Per brownie: 227 cal, 2 g prot, 220 mg sod, 54 g carb, 0.3 g fat, 0 mg chol, 3 mg calcium

- Preheat oven to 350°F. Lightly oil an 8" square baking pan.
- Add lemon juice to soy milk and set aside.
- Combine next 5 five ingredients in a medium-size bowl. Set aside.
- Cream prune butter and brown sugar in a large bowl.
- Whisk egg replacer with water until foamy and add to prune butter mixture. Blend in soy "buttermilk" mixture and vanilla.
- Add dry ingredients to liquid ingredients and mix to form batter. Fold in walnuts.
- Spread into pan and bake on upper rack of oven until toothpick inserted in center comes out clean, about 30 minutes. Cool in pan. Cut and serve.

Hint:

If adding walnuts, the fat content will go from 0.3 g to 1.8 g per brownie.

JAMMIN' Cookie Bars

*Any two of your favorite jams will complement
this scrumptious crust.*

Total Time: 45 min.
Makes 24 bars

2 1/2 cups unbleached
  all-purpose flour
1 cup wheat germ
1 cup Sucanat® or brown sugar
1/2 tsp. nutmeg
1/4 tsp. salt

1 cup Just Like Shortenin'™ (JLS)
3/4 cup fruit sweetened
  apricot jam
3/4 cup fruit sweetened
  strawberry jam

Per bar: 167 cal, 5 g prot, 53 mg sod, 37 g carb, 1 g fat, 0 mg chol, 16 mg calcium

Preheat oven to 350°F. Lightly oil a 9" x 13" baking pan.

Blend first 5 ingredients in a food processor or mixing bowl using pulse technique.

Add JLS and process to crumbly consistency. Reserve one cup of dough.

Press remaining dough along bottom and 1" up the sides of pan.

Spread apricot jam over half of dough. Spread strawberry jam over remaining half. Crumble reserved dough on top.

Bake until topping and crust are golden brown and filling is bubbly, about 25 minutes. Cool in pan. Cut and serve.

Slimmed Down Shortening

Just Like Shortenin'™ is a new product used to replace traditional high-fat shortenings. It is made from plums and apples and is becoming widely available. If this product is unavailable to you locally, refer to the "Resource Guide" on page 119 for mail order information.

No-Bake
Carob Drop Cookies

*An excellent summertime cookie when a hot stove
is the last thing on your mind.*

Total Time: 15 minutes
Makes about 5 dozen

1 1/2 cups boiling water
1 cup golden raisins
3 cups rolled oats
1/4 cup carob powder
1 tsp. cinnamon
1/2 cup chopped walnuts

1/2 cup vanilla soy milk or
   low-fat milk
2 cups brown sugar
1/4 cup natural peanut butter
1/4 cup prune butter
1/2 cup wheat germ

Per cookie: 113 cal, 4 g prot, 8 mg sod, 21 g carb, 2 g fat, 0 mg chol, 4 mg calcium

- Pour boiling water over raisins in a medium-size bowl. Set aside for 10 minutes.
- In a large bowl, combine oats, carob powder, cinnamon and walnuts.
- Drain plumped raisins and add to oat mixture.
- Warm vanilla soy milk in a medium-size saucepan over medium heat. Stir in brown sugar, peanut butter and prune butter.
- Reduce heat to low and whisk mixture until blended, about 5 minutes.
- Pour liquid over oat mixture and combine to form dough.
- Place wheat germ in a small bowl.
- Drop dough by tablespoonfuls into wheat germ and roll to coat.
- Place on cookie sheets lined with wax paper. Refrigerate until serving time.

Hint:

These cookies will be soft. For a firmer consistency, store cookies in the freezer.

Peanut Butter Cookie Bars

Topped with Creamy Carob Icing (recipe on page 88), these chewy bar cookies will be very popular around your house.

Total Time: 40 min.
Makes 24 bars

1 cup rolled oats
1 cup soy milk lite or
   low-fat milk
1 cup whole wheat pastry flour
1 tsp. baking soda
1 tsp. baking powder
1/4 tsp. salt
1/2 cup prune butter

1/4 cup chunky peanut butter
1 cup brown sugar
2 Tbsp. egg replacer }
1/2 cup cold water }
   or 1/2 cup egg white
1 tsp. vanilla extract
7/8 cup Creamy Carob Icing
   (recipe on page 88)

Per bar: 136 cal, 4 g prot, 94 mg sod, 27 g carb, 2 g fat, 0 mg chol, 35 mg calcium

Preheat oven to 350°F. Lightly oil a 9" x 13" baking pan.

Combine oats and soy milk in a small bowl. Set aside.

Sift next 4 ingredients into a medium-size bowl. Set aside.

Combine prune butter and peanut butter in a large bowl. Blend in brown sugar.

Whisk egg replacer with water until foamy and add to peanut butter mixture. Blend in vanilla and oat mixture.

Add dry ingredients to liquid ingredients and mix to form batter.

Pour into pan and bake until toothpick inserted in center comes out clean, about 20 minutes.

Cool in pan. When completely cool, frost from center to within 2" of edge. Cut and serve.

Measuring Tip
7/8 cup = 1 cup - 2 Tbsp.

Raspberry Apricot Oat Bars

Tangy apricots and zesty raspberries are the perfect
complement to a crunchy oat crust.

Total Time: 40 min.
Makes 24 bars

1 cup dried apricots
1 cup boiling water
2 cups rolled oats
1 1/2 cups unbleached
    all-purpose flour
1 cup brown sugar
1/2 cup walnuts
1 tsp. baking soda
1 tsp. cinnamon

1/4 tsp. salt
1 cup Just Like Shortenin'™ (JLS)
2/3 cup brown sugar
1 1/2 cups frozen unsweetened
    raspberries
1 tsp. almond extract
2 Tbsp. cornstarch
2 Tbsp. cold water

Per bar: 228 cal, 6 g prot, 64 mg sod, 47 g carb, 3 g fat, 0 mg chol, 17 mg calcium

- Preheat oven to 325°F. Lightly oil a 9" x 13" baking pan.
- Slice apricots and place in a small bowl with boiling water. Set aside.
- Combine next 7 ingredients in food processor or mixing bowl using pulse technique. Add JLS and process to crumbly consistency. Reserve 1 1/4 cups of crumb mixture.
- Press remaining crumb mixture into bottom of pan. Bake for 10 to 12 minutes. Set aside.
- Drain apricots, reserving 2 tablespoons of soaking liquid.
- Place apricots, reserved liquid, brown sugar and raspberries in a medium-size saucepan. Bring to a boil over medium heat. Reduce heat, add almond extract and simmer until berries are thawed, about 2 minutes.
- Dissolve cornstarch in water and add to fruit mixture. Simmer and stir until thickened, about 3 minutes. Spread into prebaked crumb crust and top with reserved crumb mixture.
- Bake until golden brown, about 15 minutes. Cool in pan. Cut and serve.

Hint:

Try frozen blueberries,
peaches or strawberries
in place of raspberries.

Great-tasting muffins don't have to be fattening. "Corny" Blueberry Muffins (recipe on page 76) are moist, fluffy and full of flavor with **just 2 grams of fat**.

Humour

Tenderness

Delight

Love

Moist and flavorful Outrageous Gingerbread (recipe on page 81) and heart-shaped Apricot Oat Scones (recipe on page 75) make breakfast treats a healthy indulgence.

Muffins & Quickbreads

Piping hot from the oven, muffins and quickbreads are as welcome after school as they are with your morning coffee or juice. These moist and rich treats are so satisfying you'll find it hard to believe they're good for you. None of the recipes uses eggs or dairy products and none contains added fat. These extraordinary muffins and quickbreads range from 61 to 215 calories and from 0.3 grams of fat to just 2 grams per serving.

Muffins and quickbreads are made without yeast, so they are easy to assemble and on the table in minutes. Even so, when I'm pressed for time, I mix the dry ingredients a few hours ahead or even the night before, and then mix and add the wet ingredients just before baking and serving. Be sure not to overmix when combining the wet and dry ingredients in these baked goods. The batter should be just a bit lumpy to yield a moist and fluffy product.

I am constantly returning to the recipes in this chapter. The tasty blend of cinnamon, orange juice and sweet apricots in Apricot Oat Scones is a consistent winner at Sunday brunch. The "Just Peachy" Muffins are my personal favorite, while Extraordinary Pumpkin Bread, featuring prune butter and chopped dates, has become a regular late-night snack for my family.

With low-fat ingredients like natural applesauce and prune butter, these wholesome treats have a longer-than-average shelf-life. They also freeze well for up to 3 months. Enjoy them anytime you like!

Applesauce Bran Muffins

Moist and delicious, these fiber-rich treats are perfect at breakfast.

Total Time: 40 min.
Makes 1 dozen

2 Tbsp. lemon juice ⎫
1 cup soy milk lite ⎬
  or 1 cup buttermilk
1 cup unbleached all-purpose flour
1 tsp. baking soda
1/4 tsp. salt
1 cup millers bran*
2 Tbsp. wheat germ
1/3 cup natural applesauce

1/3 cup liquid FruitSource®
  or brown rice syrup
2 Tbsp. egg replacer ⎫
1/2 cup cold water ⎬
  or 1/2 cup egg white
1 tsp. vanilla extract
1/2 cup golden raisins
1/4 cup Streusel Topping
  (recipe on page 96)

Per muffin: 122 cal, 4 g prot, 130 mg sod, 27 g carb, 1 g fat, 0 mg chol, 26 mg calcium

- Preheat oven to 350°F. Lightly oil muffin cups.
- Add lemon juice to soy milk and set aside.
- Sift flour, baking soda and salt into a medium-size bowl. Stir in millers bran and wheat germ. Set aside.
- Mix applesauce and FruitSource in a large bowl.
- Whisk egg replacer with water until foamy and add to applesauce mixture. Blend in vanilla and soy "buttermilk" mixture.
- Add dry ingredients to liquid ingredients, mixing just until moistened. Fold in raisins.
- Spoon into muffin cups and sprinkle with topping.
- Bake until toothpick inserted in center comes out clean, about 20 minutes. Cool in pan for 10 minutes. Remove to wire rack to cool completely.

Hint:

For a unique twist on the traditional muffin shape, try using interesting bundt-shaped muffin pans.

Apricot Oat Scones

Wonderful at breakfast or afternoon tea!

Total Time: 1 hour
Makes 1 dozen

3/4 cup dried apricots
1/2 cup boiling water
1 1/4 cups rolled oats
1 1/2 cups whole wheat
pastry flour
1/4 cup brown sugar
1 1/2 tsp. baking soda
1 tsp. baking powder
1/2 tsp. cinnamon

1/4 cup lite silken tofu
(extra firm)
1/3 cup prune butter
1/4 cup orange juice
1 tsp. vanilla extract
1/3 cup unbleached
all-purpose flour
3 Tbsp. Brown Sugar
Topping (recipe on page 86)

Per scone: 215 cal, 8 g prot, 150 mg sod, 45 g carb, 2 g fat, 0 mg chol, 37 mg calcium

Heat oven to 375°F. Lightly oil cookie sheet.

Cut apricots into thirds and place in a small bowl. Pour boiling water over apricots and set aside.

Grind oats into oat flour in food processor or blender. Place in large bowl and stir in next 5 ingredients. Set aside.

Blend tofu until smooth in food processor or mixing bowl. Blend in prune butter, orange juice and vanilla.

Add tofu mixture to dry ingredients and mix thoroughly to form dough. Drain apricots and fold into dough. Turn onto floured board.

Knead dough gently for 3 minutes, adding only enough flour to work the dough (it will be dry). Form dough into ball and flatten into disc. Place flattened dough on cookie sheet and pat into 8" circle. Score into 12 pie-shaped wedges.

Sprinkle with topping and bake until golden brown, about 30 minutes. Cool on cookie sheet for 10 minutes. Cut and serve.

Hint:

Double the recipe and serve these decorative scones at brunch.

"Corny" Blueberry Muffins

A wonderful breakfast treat, these quick and easy muffins have a long shelf life, that is, if you can keep them around!

Total Time: 30 min.
Makes 1 dozen

2 Tbsp. lemon juice ⎫
1 cup soy milk lite ⎭
   or 1 cup buttermilk
3/4 cup frozen unsweetened
   blueberries
1 1/2 cups whole wheat
   pastry flour
1/2 cup yellow cornmeal
1/4 cup wheat germ
1/4 cup Sucanat® or
   brown sugar

1 1/2 tsp. baking soda
1 tsp. baking powder
1 tsp. cinnamon
1/4 tsp. salt
1/4 cup natural applesauce
1/4 cup pure maple syrup
1 tsp. grated lemon rind
1 tsp. lemon extract
2 Tbsp. egg replacer ⎫
1/2 cup cold water ⎭
   or 1/2 cup egg white

Per muffin: 138 cal, 6 g prot, 216 mg sod, 27 g carb, 2 g fat, 0 mg chol, 53 mg calcium

- Preheat oven to 400°F. Lightly oil muffin cups.
- Add lemon juice to soy milk and set aside.
- Rinse blueberries in colander and set aside to drain.
- Combine next 8 ingredients in a medium-size bowl. Set aside.
- Mix applesauce, maple syrup, lemon rind and lemon extract in a large bowl.
- Whisk egg replacer with water until foamy and add to applesauce mixture.
- Add dry ingredients to liquid ingredients alternately with soy "buttermilk" mixture, mixing just until moistened. Gently fold in blueberries.
- Spoon into muffin cups and bake until toothpick inserted in center comes out clean, about 15 minutes. Cool in pan for 10 minutes. Remove to wire rack to cool completely.

Cranberry Upside-Down Muffins

An attractive, easy-to-make muffin that's delicious warm or cold.

Total Time: 35 min.
Makes 1 dozen

1 cup rolled oats
1 cup soy milk lite or
   low-fat milk
1 cup unbleached
   all-purpose flour
1 tsp. cinnamon
1/4 tsp. nutmeg
1 tsp. baking soda

1 tsp. baking powder
1/2 cup brown sugar
1/4 cup natural applesauce
2 Tbsp. egg replacer ⎫
1/2 cup cold water ⎭
   or 1/2 cup egg white
1 (12 oz.) can whole berry
   cranberry sauce (about 3/4 cup)

Per muffin: 170 cal, 5 g prot, 118 mg sod, 36 g carb, 2 g fat, 0 mg chol, 44 mg calcium

Preheat oven to 400°F. Lightly oil muffin cups.
Combine oats and soy milk in a large bowl. Set aside.
Sift next 5 ingredients into a medium-size bowl. Stir in brown sugar.
Add applesauce to oat mixture.
Whisk egg replacer with water until foamy and add to oat mixture.
Add dry ingredients to liquid ingredients, mixing just until moistened.
Place 2 teaspoons of cranberry sauce on bottom of each muffin cup.
Spoon batter over top, filling cups 2/3 full.
Bake until toothpick inserted in center comes out clean, about 15 minutes. Cool in pan for 10 minutes. Remove to wire rack to cool completely.

Extraordinary Pumpkin Bread

Here is a quickbread that really delivers.
It will be the star of any gathering.

Total Time: 1 hour
Serves 12

1 1/3 cups unbleached
   all-purpose flour
1 tsp. baking soda
1 tsp. baking powder
1/2 tsp. cinnamon
1/8 tsp. ground cloves
1/4 tsp. nutmeg
1/4 tsp. salt
1/2 cup prune butter

1/2 cup canned pumpkin purée
1 cup brown sugar
2 Tbsp. egg replacer }
1/2 cup cold water   }
   or 1/2 cup egg white
1/2 cup vanilla rice milk or
   low-fat milk
1/2 cup date nuggets or
   chopped dates

Per serving: 160 cal, 2 g prot, 158 mg sod, 39 g carb, 0.3 g fat, 0 mg chol, 53 mg calcium

- Preheat oven to 350°F. Lightly oil a loaf pan.
- Sift first 7 ingredients into medium-size bowl. Set aside.
- Cream prune butter and pumpkin purée in a large bowl. Blend in brown sugar.
- Whisk egg replacer with water until foamy and whisk into pumpkin mixture.
- Add dry ingredients to liquid ingredients alternately with rice milk, mixing just until moistened. Fold in dates.
- Pour into pan and bake until golden brown and toothpick inserted in center comes out clean, about 50 minutes.
- Cool in pan for 10 minutes. Remove to wire rack to cool completely.

Heavenly Banana Bread

*Enjoy this moist, delicious bread at breakfast,
lunch or as a late-night snack.*

**Total Time: 1 1/4 hours
Serves 12**

1 cup unbleached
  all-purpose flour
1 1/2 tsp. baking soda
1/2 tsp. baking powder
1 tsp. cinnamon
1/4 tsp. nutmeg
1/4 tsp. salt
1 cup millers bran
1/4 cup wheat germ
1/2 cup natural applesauce

2/3 cup liquid FruitSource®
  or brown rice syrup
2 Tbsp. egg replacer ⎫
1/2 cup cold water   ⎬
  or 1/2 cup egg white ⎭
1 tsp. vanilla extract
1 ripe banana, mashed
1/2 cup golden raisins
3/4 cup Fudgy Chocolate Glaze
  (recipe on page 92)

Per serving: 160 cal, 4 g prot, 131 mg sod, 37 g carb, 1 g fat, 0 mg chol, 66 mg calcium

- Preheat oven to 350°F. Lightly oil a loaf pan.
- Sift first 6 ingredients in a medium-size bowl. Stir in millers bran and wheat germ. Set aside.
- Mix applesauce and FruitSource in a large bowl.
- Whisk egg replacer with water until foamy and add to applesauce mixture. Stir in vanilla and banana.
- Add dry ingredients to liquid ingredients, mixing just until moistened. Fold in raisins.
- Pour into pan. Bake until golden brown and toothpick inserted in center comes out clean, about one hour.
- Remove from pan and cool on wire rack. When completely cool, top with glaze, letting drip down sides.

"Just Peachy" Muffins

Every bite is bursting with chunks of delicious fruit.

Total Time: 30 min.
Makes 1 dozen

3/4 cup dried peaches
1/2 cup boiling water
2 Tbsp. lemon juice ⎱
1 cup soy milk lite ⎰
   or 1 cup buttermilk
3/4 cup whole wheat
   pastry flour
3/4 cup unbleached
   all-purpose flour

1/4 cup wheat germ
1 1/2 tsp. baking soda
1/2 tsp. baking powder
1 tsp. cinnamon
6 Tbsp. unsweetened apple butter
3/4 cup brown sugar
2 Tbsp. egg replacer ⎱
1/2 cup cold water ⎰
   or 1/2 cup egg white

Per muffin: 173 cal, 4 g prot, 131 mg sod, 40 g carb, 0.9 g fat, 0 mg chol, 43 mg calcium

- Preheat oven to 350°F. Lightly oil muffin cups.
- Cut peaches into thirds and place in a small bowl. Pour boiling water over peaches and set aside.
- Add lemon juice to soy milk and set aside.
- Combine next 6 ingredients in a medium-size bowl. Set aside.
- Cream apple butter and brown sugar in a large bowl.
- Whisk egg replacer with water until foamy and add to apple butter mixture.
- Add dry ingredients to liquid ingredients alternately with soy "buttermilk" mixture, mixing just until moistened. Drain peaches and fold into batter.
- Spoon into muffin cups and bake in upper third of oven until top springs back when touched and muffins are golden, about 12 minutes.
- Cool in pan for 10 minutes. Remove to wire rack to cool completely.

Outrageous Gingerbread

There's only one thing to say about this gingerbread:
It's outrageous!

Total Time: 1 hour
Serves 16

2 Tbsp. lemon juice ⎱
1 cup soy milk lite ⎰
   or 1 cup buttermilk
2 cups whole wheat
   pastry flour
1/4 cup wheat germ
2 tsp. baking soda
2 tsp. cinnamon
1 tsp. baking powder
1 tsp. ginger powder

1/2 tsp. nutmeg
1/2 tsp. salt
1/4 tsp. ground cloves
3/4 cup prune butter
2 cups brown sugar
2 Tbsp. egg replacer ⎱
1/2 cup cold water ⎰
   or 1/2 cup egg white
1 Tbsp. grated fresh gingerroot
1/2 tsp. grated lemon rind

Per serving: 194 cal, 3 g prot, 217 mg sod, 45 g carb, 0.8 g fat, 0 mg chol, 67 mg calcium

- Preheat oven to 400°F. Lightly oil a 9" x 13" baking pan.
- Add lemon juice to soy milk and set aside.
- Combine next 9 ingredients in a medium-size bowl. Set aside.
- Cream prune butter and brown sugar in a large bowl.
- Whisk egg replacer with water and add to prune butter mixture. Blend in gingerroot and lemon rind.
- Add dry ingredients to liquid ingredients alternately with soy "buttermilk" mixture, mixing just until moistened.
- Pour into pan, place in oven and immediately reduce oven temperature to 375°F.
- Bake until toothpick inserted in center comes out clean, about 30 minutes. Cool in pan, cut and serve.

Pumpkin Raisin Muffins

*Golden raisins, cinnamon and nutmeg add a touch
of spice to these rich-tasting treats.*

**Total Time: 30 min.
Makes 1 dozen**

1 cup whole wheat pastry flour
1/4 cup wheat germ
1/2 tsp. baking soda
1 tsp. baking powder
1 tsp. cinnamon
1/4 tsp. nutmeg
1/8 tsp. ground cloves
1/4 tsp. salt
1/2 cup prune butter

1/2 cup canned pumpkin purée
1 cup brown sugar
2 Tbsp. egg replacer ⎫
1/2 cup cold water ⎭
  or 1/2 cup egg white
1/2 tsp. vanilla extract
1/4 cup soy milk lite or
  low-fat milk
1/2 cup golden raisins

Per muffin: 61 cal, 3 g prot, 127 mg sod, 37 g carb, 0.8 g fat, 0 mg chol, 71 mg calcium

- Preheat oven to 350°F. Lightly oil muffin cups.
- Combine first 8 ingredients in a medium-size bowl. Set aside.
- Cream prune butter and pumpkin purée in a large bowl. Blend in brown sugar.
- Whisk egg replacer with water until foamy and add to pumpkin mixture. Blend in vanilla.
- Add dry ingredients to liquid ingredients alternately with soy milk, mixing just until moistened. Fold in raisins.
- Spoon into muffin cups and bake until golden and a toothpick inserted in center comes out clean, about 15 minutes. Cool in pan for 10 minutes. Remove to wire rack to cool completely.

Raisin Bran Muffins

*Maple syrup adds just the right amount
of sweetness to this fiber-rich treat.*

**Total Time: 30 min.
Makes 1 dozen**

1 1/4 cups unbleached
   all-purpose flour
1 tsp. baking soda
1 tsp. cinnamon
1/2 tsp. baking powder
1/4 tsp. salt
6 Tbsp. whole wheat pastry flour
1/2 cup millers bran
6 Tbsp. natural applesauce

6 Tbsp. pure maple syrup
1 1/2 Tbsp. egg replacer }
6 Tbsp. water
  or 6 Tbsp. egg white
1/2 tsp. vanilla extract
1/2 cup soy milk lite or
  low-fat milk
2 1/2 Tbsp. Brown Sugar Topping
  (recipe on page 86)

Per muffin: 103 cal, 2 g prot, 142 mg sod, 24 g carb, 0.4 g fat, 0 mg chol, 33 mg calcium

- Preheat oven to 350°F. Lightly oil muffin pan.
- Sift first 5 ingredients in a medium-size bowl. Stir in whole wheat flour and millers bran. Set aside.
- In a large bowl, combine applesauce and maple syrup.
- Whisk egg replacer with water until foamy and add to applesauce mixture. Whisk in vanilla and soy milk.
- Add dry ingredients to liquid ingredients, mixing just until moistened.
- Spoon into prepared muffin cups and sprinkle with topping.
- Bake until toothpick inserted in center comes out clean, about 15 minutes. Cool in pan for 10 minutes. Transfer to wire rack to cool completely.

Hint:

For a heartier muffin, substitute whole wheat flour for the all-purpose flour and wheat germ for the 6 tablespoons whole wheat pastry flour called for in the original.

Zucchini Streusel Muffins

Moist, wholesome and delicious!

Total Time: 30 min.
Makes 1 dozen

1 Tbsp. lemon juice ⎫
1/2 cup soy milk lite ⎭
   or 1/2 cup buttermilk
1 cup whole wheat
   pastry flour
1/4 cup oat bran
2 Tbsp. wheat germ
1 1/2 tsp. baking soda
1 tsp. baking powder
1/2 tsp. cinnamon
1/8 tsp. salt

6 Tbsp. Sucanat® or
   brown sugar
1/4 cup natural applesauce
2 Tbsp. egg replacer ⎫
1/2 cup cold water ⎭
   or 1/2 cup egg white
1 tsp. grated lemon rind
1 cup shredded zucchini
3/4 cup golden raisins
2 Tbsp. Streusel Topping
   (recipe on page 96)

Per muffin: 120 cal, 4 g prot, 184 mg sod, 26 g carb, 1 g fat, 0 mg chol, 58 mg calcium

- Preheat oven to 350°F. Lightly oil muffin cups.
- Add lemon juice to soy milk and set aside.
- Combine next 8 ingredients in a medium-size bowl. Set aside.
- Place applesauce in a large bowl.
- Whisk egg replacer with water until foamy and add to applesauce. Whisk in lemon rind and soy "buttermilk" mixture.
- Add dry ingredients to liquid ingredients, mixing just until moistened. Fold in zucchini and raisins.
- Spoon into muffin cups and sprinkle with topping.
- Bake until toothpick inserted in center comes out clean, about 15 minutes. Cool in pan for 10 minutes. Remove to wire rack to cool completely.

Hint:

For a delicious party treat, bake these in mini-muffin pans.

Icings, Fillings & Toppings

While some cakes need no embellishment other than a sprinkling of powdered sugar, the right icing, filling or topping can turn a good cake into a centerpiece. Unfortunately, the icing on the cake can be the most sinful part. Traditional icings are loaded with refined confectioners' sugar, high-fat butter, cream or shortening, and sometimes artificial flavoring. Boiled icings are made with egg whites.

But rest easy! None of those guilt-ridden ingredients are used here. Instead, these recipes call for friendly ingredients like fruit juice concentrate and agar flakes to create rich and creamy, guiltless icings. Agar is a natural gelling agent that works like a charm in desserts. For custard-like fillings, I use FruitSource® or pure maple syrup in combination with lite silken tofu and vanilla rice milk. You will be amazed by the taste and most of the recipes take only 10 minutes to complete.

You'll also find nutty spice toppings and flavorful fruit toppings to add pizazz to cobblers, puddings and pies. As with the icings, each recipe is cross-referenced to indicate complementary recipes in other chapters of the book. The amount indicated in each recipe is scaled for the complementary recipe referred to. But feel free to mix and match, creating your own luscious, low-fat desserts.

The recipes here range from 0 grams of fat to only 2 grams per serving. And none has over 99 calories per serving. The secret is simple: no eggs and no dairy. For any unfamiliar ingredients, refer to the "Glossary" on page 13. For more information on icing yields and frosting techniques, refer to "Techniques" on page 11.

Blueberry Topping

This versatile topping is picture perfect on Blueberry Custard Pie (recipe on page 39).

Total Time: 10 min.
  Makes 3 cups

*3/4 cup frozen apple juice
  concentrate
2 cups frozen blueberries*

*2 Tbsp. cornstarch
2 Tbsp. cold water*

Per serving (1/4 cup): 27 cal, 0.2 g prot, 3 mg sod, 7 g carb, 0.1 g fat, 0 mg chol, 2 mg calcium

- Bring juice concentrate to a boil in a small saucepan.
- Reduce heat and add blueberries. Simmer and stir until blueberries are thawed, about 5 minutes.
- Dissolve cornstarch in water and add to fruit mixture. Simmer and stir until thickened, about 3 minutes.
- Top dessert and proceed with recipe.

Brown Sugar Topping

This quick and tasty recipe tops a dozen muffins or scones.

Total Time: 40 min.
  Makes 1 dozen

*2 Tbsp. brown sugar
1/2 tsp. cinnamon
1/4 tsp. nutmeg*

Per serving (1/2 tsp.): 9 cal, 0 g prot, .7 mg sod, 2 g carb, 0 g fat, 0 mg chol, 3 mg calcium

- Combine all ingredients in a small bowl.
- Sprinkle on muffins or scones and proceed with recipe.

Chocolate Raspberry Icing

Try this fluffy, deep chocolate frosting on Chocolate Raspberry Roll
(recipe on page 24).

Total Time: 10 min.
Makes 2 1/3 cups

1/2 cup frozen raspberry juice
  concentrate
3 rounded Tbsp. agar flakes

1 (10.5 oz.) pkg. lite silken tofu
  (extra firm)
1/4 cup cocoa powder
1 tsp. almond extract

Per serving (3 Tbsp.): 23 cal, 2 g prot, 27 mg sod, 2 g carb, 0.5 g fat, 0 mg chol, 8 mg calcium

Bring juice concentrate to a boil in a small saucepan.
Sprinkle in agar and reduce heat to low. Simmer and stir until
thickened, about 3 minutes. Remove from heat and set aside.
Blend tofu until smooth in food processor or mixing bowl.
Blend in cocoa and almond extract.
Add thickened juice to tofu mixture and process until smooth.
Spread on cooled cake and refrigerate to set.

Hint:

*Try Dole® Country
Raspberry juice
concentrate. It is a
delicious blend of apple,
pineapple, grape and
raspberry juices.*

Cinnamon Almond Crunch

This sweet and crunchy topping is especially tasty
on baked puddings or sprinkled over frozen desserts.

Total Time: 5 min.
Makes about 1/4 cup

1/4 cup almonds, chopped
1/4 tsp. cinnamon

1/8 tsp. nutmeg
4 tsp. Sucanat® or brown sugar

Per serving (1/4 Tbsp.): 21 cal, 0.5 g prot, 19 mg sod, 2 g carb, 2 g fat, 0 mg chol, 10 mg calcium

In a food processor or blender, blend all ingredients until crumbly.
Sprinkle on your favorite dessert and proceed with recipe.

Cinnamon Cobbler Topping

This topping takes the cake on Spirited Peach Cobbler (recipe on page 51)

Total Time: 10 min.
Makes 1 1/2 cups

1/2 cup whole wheat pastry flour
1/4 cup wheat germ
1/3 cup Sucanat® or brown sugar

3 Tbsp. walnuts, chopped
1 tsp. cinnamon
3 Tbsp. Just Like Shortenin'™ (JLS)

Per serving (2 Tbsp.): 99 cal, 4 g prot, 14 mg sod, 17 g carb, 2 g fat, 0 mg chol, 20 mg calcium

- Blend first 5 ingredients in food processor or mixing bowl, using pulse technique
- Add JLS and blend until crumbly.
- Top dessert and proceed with recipe.

Creamy Carob Icing

This rich-tasting icing is both fat and cholesterol free! Delicious on cupcakes or Peanut Butter Cookie Bars (recipe on page 69).

Total Time: 5 min.
Makes 7/8 cup

1/4 cup carob powder
1/4 cup brown sugar

3 Tbsp. tapioca flour or arrowroot
3 Tbsp. warm soy milk lite

Per serving (1 Tbsp.): 22 cal, 0.1 g prot, 2 mg sod, 5 g carb, 0 g fat, 0 mg chol, 9 mg calcium

- In a small bowl, combine carob and brown sugar, pressing out lumps with a fork. Stir in flour.
- Pour warm soy milk over carob mixture and stir until smooth.
- Spread on cooled dessert and refrigerate to set.

Hints:

For Creamy Chocolat Icing, use cocoa powde instead of carob powder.
Double this recipe to i a single layer cake.